T0129311

LIVE WORK SHINE

How to Use Time for What Matters

ROWENA HUBBLE

BALBOA.PRESS

A DIVISION OF HAY HOUSE

Copyright © 2019 Rowena Hubble.

All rights reserved. No part of this book may be used or reproduced by any means, graphic, electronic, or mechanical, including photocopying, recording, taping or by any information storage retrieval system without the written permission of the author except in the case of brief quotations embodied in critical articles and reviews.

Balboa Press books may be ordered through booksellers or by contacting:

Balboa Press
A Division of Hay House
1663 Liberty Drive
Bloomington, IN 47403
www.balboapress.com.au
1 (877) 407-4847

Because of the dynamic nature of the Internet, any web addresses or links contained in this book may have changed since publication and may no longer be valid. The views expressed in this work are solely those of the author and do not necessarily reflect the views of the publisher, and the publisher hereby disclaims any responsibility for them.

The author of this book does not dispense medical advice or prescribe the use of any technique as a form of treatment for physical, emotional, or medical problems without the advice of a physician, either directly or indirectly. The intent of the author is only to offer information of a general nature to help you in your quest for emotional and spiritual well-being. In the event you use any of the information in this book for yourself, which is your constitutional right, the author and the publisher assume no responsibility for your actions.

Any people depicted in stock imagery provided by Getty Images are models, and such images are being used for illustrative purposes only. Certain stock imagery © Getty Images.

Print information available on the last page.

ISBN: 978-1-5043-1988-1 (sc)
ISBN: 978-1-5043-1987-4 (e)

Balboa Press rev. date: 03/17/2020

♥

Thank you to everyone who has played a
part in allowing me to share my passion of
optimising time to live, work and shine.

To Nick, Mitch and Layton you are my everything.

And Donna you continue to inspire
me to find joy in every day.
I feel your presence from above. You
will be forever in my heart.

Contents

Preface   i

Introduction   1
My Story   6
The Problem with the 40 Hour Work Week   12

Part 1 – The Power of Your Mindset   23
   The Power of Desire and Belief   24
   Happiness Makes a Huge Difference   37
   How to Focus and Stop Procrastinating   50
   The Secret to Developing Good Habits   60

Part 2 – How to Structure Your Day   70
   Starting Your Day Well   71
   Prioritising Your Most Important Tasks   78
   Managing Your Energy Levels   89
   Why This One Family Ritual
   Must be Given Priority   98

Part 3 – Managing Your Time Thieves   105
   Why You Must Stop Conscious Multi-Tasking   106
   Manage Your Inbox So It Doesn't Manage You   113
   How to Improve the Effectiveness of Meetings   122
   Why Less is More   127

Conclusion   141
References   143

Preface

Why I wrote this book

During my many years in corporate life, which you will read about in the chapter "My Story," I have successfully juggled the game of life and work. While at times it hasn't been easy, I have ensured I've stayed true to my values and clear on my priorities. I've been a daughter, a sister, a wife, a mum, a friend, a community volunteer and corporate executive.

I've worked in a number of different organisations and at each one have managed to never be too busy (it's just not part of my vocabulary). I have never worked long hours, been there for all I have wanted to for my family and friends, maintained good health and fitness and continued to progress in my career. Unfortunately, many people who have worked around me, both more junior, my peers and more senior co-workers have been overwhelmed by the "I'm too busy" epidemic. They have been unable to manage the juggle, often working long hours and sacrificing time for one's own health and well-being – not to mention valuable time with family and friends.

Everyone has an abundance of reasons why they can't manage their life-work juggle whether that be "the boss expects too much" or "the kids just keep demanding more and more of me." For a small minority these reasons are out of one's control, but for most of us, they are simply excuses. And sure, I too have had my share of excuses at times – I'm not perfect. But for the most part, I have mastered the art of balancing life and work.

It doesn't matter who you are, or the position you hold in your organisation, I feel very confident that you too can create a healthy life-work balance.

What I am inviting you to do is to ask yourself some rather tough questions...

Are you truly a victim of circumstances or are your circumstances a victim of you? I challenge you that there is a way to manage your circumstances no matter what those circumstances are right now.

Where there is a will, there is a way – it is within your reach. If you really want it, you'll find a way – if you don't, you'll find excuses.

I have written this book to help you with the life-work juggle and to support a shift in this societal epidemic of being too busy. My goal is to help people maximise their effectiveness, balance their home and work priorities, generate outstanding results and live a happy life. And my hope is that you will be one of these people too.

Is this book for you

Are you finding it hard to manage everything you want to do at work and at home? Are you consistently feeling too busy and not sure how to get on top of things? Is this feeling impacting your mental or physical health and your relationships?

If your answer is yes to any of these questions, then this book is for you.

If you have a job, whether that be at the start or end of your career, in junior roles, middle management or senior management, this book is for you. It's a great resource for you regardless of whether you are an office-based employee, work in a factory, work for yourself or work for an employer.

How to use this book

Think of this book as a reference guide. Each chapter provides an overview of some big topics – entire books have been written on each of these topics. But in this book, the main principles and the best information has been gleaned from all of that so that you won't need to spend weeks or months reading lots of time-management books.

This book introduces topics around re-shaping your workday and at the end of each chapter there are thought-provoking check-point questions ❷ to ask yourself. Then, it suggests some action steps ❿ to take in order to make a step change. But step change takes time and you can't do everything at once.

I would suggest that at first, you read the book cover to cover – it's short so it won't take that long. Then, reflect on what are your areas of opportunity and what is the number one area that would make the biggest impact on your life. Focus on that one area for a month or more until you have made it a habit.

Once you have mastered one area that you choose to work on and do it often enough, so it becomes a habit, then turn to area number two and repeat. Then, do it again with the next area of opportunity and repeat. For example, if you know that your priority is needing help with how you start your day, focus on your mornings until you establish a good, solid habit. And then, work on the next area that you want to improve.

I would also suggest that you find an accountability partner, a friend or work colleague, who can help you stay on track in order to make the required change.

Once you start to free time up for yourself, you'll be amazed at how much better your life will become. You'll finally have some breathing room to do the things that are the most important to you. By using your time for what matters you will be able to live, work and shine.

How does that sound to you? Sound good?

If yes, let's not waste another precious minute!

Introduction

It's the beginning of another workday. You get up and pour your coffee into your favourite mug. Today, you have an extremely important meeting at 9 am that could mean the difference between getting a promotion or not...

But then, your five-year-old daughter wakes up and cries out in pain. Quickly, you put your coffee mug down, run into her room and see that she looks really sick. You put your hand on her tiny forehead and it's as hot as the coffee you just sipped...

Your heart sinks as you think of the meeting you had at 9. What do you do now? Can you get someone else to look after your daughter? But how can you abandon your child at such a time as this? Your stress level peaks as you consider your options.

You too have probably had a very similar event happen in your life. It's the struggle we all face – juggling to balance life and work.

Unforeseen sickness. Impossible deadlines. New tasks and projects piled up on your already demanding workload. And constantly changing priorities. You're simply overwhelmed by all of it, feeling buried in things to do and drained of the capacity to do them. The "busyness" routine often results in sacrificing important areas of your life, such as family, friends, physical and emotional health, in exchange for sheer hard work.

If you can relate to this, you are not alone. This describes how the average person feels.

A healthy balance, a healthy integration of life and work is something that we all desire to achieve in the workplace without sacrificing quality time for our family, friends, interests and passions. However, for many of us, this unfortunately seems like an unrealistic dream...

But can this dream become a reality? Is there a solution? Is there any way out of the chaos? Is this the way that it has to be? Or is it a choice?

And in today's competitive market, is it possible to attain a healthy integration of life and work without risking losing your job, or that next promotion, over it?

The answer is a resounding YES.

There is a way. It is possible. And I can show you how...

With a renewed focus on your mindset and spending time on what matters a healthy life-work integration can be a reality.

Whilst caring for people in the end stages of life, a palliative care nurse, Bronnie Ware, recorded the regrets of her patients, documented in her book, *Top 5 Regrets of the Dying*. The most stated regrets were:

"I wish I...

1. had the courage to live a life true to myself, not the life others expected of me.
2. hadn't worked so hard.
3. had the courage to express my feelings.
4. had stayed in touch with friends.
5. had let myself be happier."

The number two regret was that they wished they hadn't worked so hard. By doing so, they had missed their children's youth and their partner's companionship. Ms. Ware wrote: "The people I nursed deeply regretted spending so much of their lives on the treadmill of a work existence."

This regret is not surprising to any of us. It's a regret that perhaps you are feeling today. It was unfortunately too late for these elderly people; however, it's not too late for you.

Ask yourself, what are the important areas of your life? What is truly important to you? What do you want to be known for and always remembered for? And does this reflect your reality today? If not, then you may find this book to be invaluable. After all, one of the worst things that could happen to you is that you get to the end of your life and regret the way you lived it.

The argument for not being able to satisfy the above wishes is often that the working days, weeks and years consume too much of our time, so we can't meet our personal desires. For most of us, the obsession with work is about having enough money to meet and satisfy the needs and wants of ourselves and our families.

So, how can we be more productive in life, work less and still have a comfortable lifestyle?

That is what this book will cover...

It doesn't mean that you need to work harder; it's not about working harder but working smarter. Working smarter means that you value your time more than before, making your waking hours more productive and more effective. This may include depositing new tools into your productivity tool kit, including setting priorities and sticking to them, creating new habits, focusing on a singular task instead of multi-tasking, and recognising how to maximise your energy levels.

All of this is covered in this book...

To have it all, most of us need to make some changes. These changes will ensure that you are in control and are no longer constantly on the busy roller coaster of life. You have to accept that expecting to achieve a different outcome, without investing in change, will result in no change. As Henry Ford famously said, "**If you do what you've always done, you'll get what you've always got**."

The content in this book is common-sense and logical, but common-sense and logical in ways that aren't being practised widely today. It's my personal guarantee that you will come away with some new tools, techniques and direction that will allow you to achieve a healthy balance between life and work. And that when you implement the advice in this book, you too will be able to escape the often-vicious cycle of life.

I challenge you to reshape your everyday routine and allow yourself to achieve all that you desire. You can't replay the key events in your life that really matter. And this is why you have to ask yourself the question, what is more important? The love that you show to a sick child who has a fever or making a meeting that may not make any difference in your life anyway? What would your child think? What will she remember?

If you manage your time and energy wisely, then you won't miss out on those most important moments of life with your loved ones. And compared to many, you won't feel over-worked only to regret it later.

You can have it all! It's not that easy, but if you implement the simple strategies given in this book, life-work balance will not only be a possibility, but a certainty.

The question is, are you ready? Are you ready to make the choice to take control of your life?

The real secret of getting ahead is simply getting started... Let today be the start of a new tomorrow for you.

My Story

For many people, the pressures of life and work build over time until they reach a near crisis point. There is an aha moment, a trigger point that forces them to reassess where they are in life. They begin to question what toll their daily life is having on their mental and physical health and whether they can continue to operate this way. Perhaps that is where you find yourself to be today...

That's the story for most people, and that's why I've written this book. Fortunately for me, my story is quite different. For me, what started soon after leaving high school quickly became a good habit that has held me in great stead. While it hasn't been easy, I've managed the juggling game of life and work and never been too busy. And, I'm happy to say that I've continued to achieve a healthy integration of life and work to this day.

As mentioned, my journey of managing life and work started in my late teen years, out of sheer necessity. I was working full time and commenced my university degree. Like many part-time students, I attended university three nights a week from 6 pm to 9 pm. The other nights were dedicated to assignments, study, etc. That meant leaving work on time every night. But I wanted to be a high performer at work, too. I had the belief that I could do both and made choices accordingly.

Being young and naïve, I didn't think about or probably even know the perceived culture that exists in some workplaces (and, on reflection, existed in the company I was at) that you needed to be seen in the office beyond the standard working hours to climb the corporate ladder. All I knew was that I had lots of work to get done and only a limited time to do it.

I soon became known as Miss Effectiveness by removing inefficiencies which helped me to make each day as productive as possible. Not that I knew it at the time, but I was practicing the principles of the 80/20 Rule and Parkinson's Law (expanded upon in subsequent chapters). I focused on the 20 percent of effort that provided 80 percent of the productive outcomes and restricted the time I had to get the work done, and got it done.

When I changed jobs part way through my undergraduate degree, I used the same tools and techniques from my productivity toolkit – the exact same tools you will learn from this book. Implementing these practices, I was able to replicate my nine-to-five achievement of life-work balance and graduated from University in record time. In addition, I was promoted to middle management by the time I was degree qualified.

With this recipe for achievement, why would I change my approach post graduating? Why would I revert to the all-so-familiar habits of others in the workforce of working long hours?

I continued to pack up and leave the office at 5 pm or 5.30 pm post my degree. If anyone in the office were to remark,

I'd say I was doing post grad studies (which I was) or putting the finishing touches to the new house my husband and I had moved into (which I was). Externally, I occasionally needed to provide the reason why I left work on time but internally I knew no explanation was needed. I got through my work and more and was living proof that *you don't do a good job if your job is all you do!*

I was in my mid-twenties and thought I had this balance thing all worked out, when the greatest events of my life occurred – the birth of my beautiful boys, now young men. Mitch was born first and then, two years later, Layton. And, as for any parent, you know that a child will turn your whole life upside down – an incredibly positive upside down, but nevertheless upside down! Now, I not only needed to juggle work and interests outside of work, but also the love, care and nurturing of two other human beings.

I was envious of the mums or dads who were content to take twelve months or more off work to care for their children. Unfortunately, I wasn't so content and missed the stimulation of the work environment, but yep, you guessed it; I wanted to have my cake and eat it too. I wanted to work, but I wanted to be there for my boys. And, I didn't want to miss out on all those milestones – from newborn till today. I started working from home a lot, and worked out that, with focus, working from home can be as effective, and often more effective, than being present in the office.

When Mitch and Layton were three and one, we moved to a new home. We hadn't planned ahead for the move, and hence, hadn't planned ahead for child-care spots close to our new home. Finding child-care was incredibly difficult, and it was before the days of nannies other than for the very wealthy. Most centres didn't have vacancies, and for those that did, there was a reason (not a good reason) they did!

We found a suitable child-care centre, but with one catch: its hours were 8 am to 4 pm. The proximity of the child-care centre, relative to my workplace, made sense for me to do the drop off and pick up. The child-care centre was only about twenty minutes from work, but that would mean a maximum workday in the office of 8.20 am to 3.40 pm. It was at that point that both I, and the company I worked for, had a tough decision to make. I either worked 8.20 am to 3.40 pm in the office or I didn't work at all.

I committed to my employer that the work would get done, and fortunately, they were willing to take the risk and see how things would go. From that day and for the next four years, I finished work at 3.40 pm each and every day (working three and then four days per week in the office), with additional hours of work from home each evening.

Flexibility in the workplace is a joint partnership requiring commitment from both the employer and the employee. There needs to be "give and take" to ensure the job gets done and results delivered. I ensured throughout my time of working different hours to the 9 to 5, five days a week, that I was flexible where needed.

Two years into my 3.40 pm finish years, I was appointed Financial Controller of McDonald's Australia. At that time, I was part of the senior leadership team and had a team of about fifty employees working within my team. Yes, there were days that it was tough, really tough, to race out the office door at 3.40 pm. It took a lot of co-ordination and discipline, but I had no choice. If I wasn't at child-care at 4 pm to pick up my boys, there would be a financial penalty. But the financial penalty was nothing in comparison to the "mum penalty," the guilt of my children thinking Mummy wasn't coming.

In addition to the "mum guilt" I'd be lying if I said there was no guilt leaving the office when my boss, my peers and my team were still working away. But to me, spending quality time with my children was much more important than the temporary guilt that I felt about leaving work early. Temporary because I was very confident that the work was getting done and getting done with no impact on quality.

Post the preschool days, I was adamant I wanted to be there for all those important things in my children's lives – whether that be reading groups, sports carnivals, musical performances, charity days or school community involvement. And I'm very proud to say, I've been there for most. I recall a day that I was torn between going to work and taking a day's leave to attend a school event. I recall someone saying, "In years to come, you won't remember having attended a particular work meeting or day in the office, but you will always remember attending that special event in your child's life. And, they will always remember you being there, too." Reflecting years later, that was great advice.

You may say I was fortunate to have the sort of job that provided flexibility. But in reality, it was a choice. There were plenty around me, actually, most around me, who could have also made that choice themselves, but didn't. I agree that in some jobs, it's just not possible; but in most corporate roles, with lots of organisation and effectiveness, the choice is there. You know the saying, "you make your own luck?" I think this applies here, too. It's up to you.

Since my early working years, I've ensured I've stayed true to what I believe – it's not the hours of work that you put in that counts, but what you do in those hours. And as stated earlier-you don't do a good job if your job is all you do.

Today, I no longer have the demands of part-time study or young children. My boys are now young adults, but it is very rare to see me in the office past 5.30 pm. Today, the child-care demands are replaced by a goal to run a marathon, volunteer at various events, or simply to be home to have dinner with the family.

Sure, in all these years, I've done my fair share of work at night from the comfort of my home. But it has allowed me to have it all – a career, sharing all those milestones with my family, good health, and community involvement. And, I wouldn't change it for the world.

That's my story. But it could be yours too. There is no reason why you cannot do what I have done. Most of us don't realise that it's more of a choice than not. More and more organisations understand that a happy employee is one who has a healthy life-work balance, so they are more accommodating now than ever before. But you have to have the right mindset and tools, and that's what you're going to learn in this book...

But before we get into how to have the right mindset and all of the tools, let's first cover the problem with the 40-hour work week. You'll be surprised to find out why it's obsolete and needs to be changed...

The Problem with the 40 Hour Work Week

Have you ever wondered why most of the world works a 40-hour work week? Who made that decision? And why? What is the problem with it? And should it be changed?

Let's get to it...

The Monday to Friday working week, from around 9 am to 5 pm, is the norm for the majority of salaried workers; and, it's been the norm for almost a century. Putting aside the fact that many of us work much more than the 35 to 40-hour week for now, why has the 9 am to 5 pm tradition remained for so long?

If we look back in history, during the Industrial Revolution, factories needed to run around the clock. So, employees during this era frequently worked 10 to 16-hour days. In the 1920s, however, it was Henry Ford, founder of Ford Motor Company, who challenged the longer day. He was one of the first employers to establish the five-day, 40-hour work week.

The Ford Motor Company not only reduced their working day to eight hours, but doubled their workers' pay at the same time. The shorter day coupled with a higher pay rate resulted in a spike in productivity. Within two years of implementing this change, profit margins doubled.

Moreover, Ford sought to promote an ideal home life for its employees. Company executives believed that, in order to live properly, every man should have more time to spend with his family. At Ford's own admission, however, the expectation on workers was higher with the move to the five-day work week. Although workers' time on the job had decreased, they were expected to expend more effort while they were there; and they did.

The Ford Motor Company results paved the way for other companies to adopt the shorter workday of eight hours. The 40-hour work-week, however, has remained largely the same for most of us ever since.

Swedish Case Study

The Swedes are taking the lead in a new era of change.

Sweden has long been a laboratory for initiatives to strike a better life-work balance, recognising that treating workers well is positive for the bottom line. The six-hour workday, or 30-hour work week, has become a staple of the nation's socially progressive initiatives.

A number of Swedish companies that have reduced the working day to a six-hour day have found results similar to the Ford Motor company. The same or more work gets done in a shorter time period, and employees are happier. "I think the eight-hour workday is not as effective as one would think," the CEO of a Swedish app development company has commented.

"We thought doing a shorter work week would mean we'd have to hire more, but it hasn't resulted in that because everyone works more efficiently," said Maria Brath, who founded a start-up in Stockholm based on a six-hour day. "Today we get more done in six hours than comparable companies do in eight," she continued. "We believe it comes with the high level of creativity demanded in this line of work. We believe nobody can be creative and productive in eight hours straight. Six hours is more reasonable, even though we too, of course, check Facebook or the news at times."

The shorter working day has challenged teams to constantly find new ways to do more with the available time, more effectively utilising time e.g. not sending unnecessary emails or time consumed in meetings. Everyone is conscious of not wasting time – both their own and those of others. They are conscious of using time for what matters.

A Swedish Toyota vehicle service centre transitioned to a six-hour day back in 2002. This change was introduced to address employee stress and customer complaints concerning long waiting times. The change resulted in employees doing, as a minimum, the same amount within the six-hour workday and often more than they did in the eight-hour day. More time away from work has meant employees are more efficient and happier on the job.

Over the span of about a year, a Swedish retirement home (Svartedalens) conducted an experiment for nurses to work six-hour days while receiving a salary for eight-hour days. This was part of a study enacted by the Swedish government to observe whether a shorter workday might yield increased productivity on the job. A published report concluded that, in its first year, this program's six-hour workday had dramatically reduced absenteeism, plus enhanced both productivity and workers' health.

Data from the project over a year's time, which compared Svartedalens' staff with employees of a control group at a similar facility, demonstrated clearly that 68 nurses who worked six-hour days took 50% fewer sick days. The nurses were 20% happier, which is not surprising. In addition, they reported having more energy. This new-found energy allowed them to perform 64% more activities with elderly residents, which was one of the metrics researchers utilised to measure productivity. The residents of the nursing home noticed the positive impact too, saying that the standard of care was higher.

At Gothenburg's Sahlgrenska University Hospital, one of the largest in Europe, a similar approach has been used to counter both burnout and high absenteeism and the results were very positive. Surgery waiting times were reduced from months to weeks, allowing patients to return to work faster, ultimately reducing sick leave in workplaces and boosting the economy. On an individual level employees had increased energy levels, having time for rest and, importantly, time for their family and friends.

The Swedish study isn't the first one that connected happier, rested workers and better outcomes for employers. A 2014 Stanford University research paper confirmed there is a non-linear relationship between hours worked and output. In fact, research has shown that too much work can lead to damaged productivity.

Whilst there is strong evidence from the Swedish companies moving to a six-hour day, showing that productivity can definitely increase with fewer hours worked, the transition to a shorter working week or even a change from the 9 to 5 mentality, is moving very slowly. In many to most companies today, there is still the mentality that we need to be visible in the office during the 9 to 5 working day, five days a week. Beyond the 9 to 5, there is a common perception that working long hours signals dedication. It may signal dedication, in the eyes of some, but it certainly doesn't signal greater productivity.

What makes a workplace or individual successful is not the total number of hours worked; instead, it's about getting the job done. The problem is that many focus only on the "hours worked" component, and that's not the best metric for productivity.

Putting overtime aside for a moment, let's say that giving all employees the same schedule and the same number of hours may seem like an equitable system. However, it presumes we are all the same, our work patterns are the same (the same each and every day) and we all need the same hours to achieve the required outcomes. The reality is that this presumption results in less than optimal productivity, decreased output, and ultimately the compromised satisfaction and happiness of employees.

There are a number of issues to consider when we all have the same schedule, each and every workday:

- **Individual peak productivity** – Not everyone works the same. Some people are at their most effective first thing in the morning, but by mid-afternoon, they are ready for a long break. Others may prefer to sleep in and work later into the evening. The 9 to 5 schedule means we all need to conform to being "on" as much as possible during 9 to 5.

Based on survey data, most of us reach our peak of productivity on Tuesday and experience a low on Friday. But we are required to work the same hours each day of the week. Why not work a little longer on a Tuesday whilst productivity is high? And, on a Friday, why not finish the working day early? In reality, little productive work is usually done in those last few hours on a Friday by many workers. Finishing earlier on a Friday may also be the motivator needed to accomplish more on the last working day of the week.

- **Workload variables** – There are days when 10 hours are required in a workday to meet a deadline or get a task completed. Understandably, on these days, you may be expected to work overtime; and normally, unpaid overtime. There are also other times when 5 hours is all that is needed to complete the day's tasks. Whilst the hours of work are adjusted for overtime, they are often not adjusted in the opposite direction – when the required output is achieved in fewer hours, there is still the expectation to work the "full" working day. This doesn't make a lot of sense.

- **Creative stimulation** – Innovation is driven by the new – new ideas, new situations, new environments and new perspectives. Creativity is challenged when the working hours and working environment each day of the week don't change.

- **Travelling time** – Travelling an hour, both to and from work, is probably close to the norm. That's 10 hours a week – or more than one full workday! Travelling is not only a big consumer of the limited resource of time, but it also can be draining mentally and physically, keeping us from achieving output – whether that is work productivity or addressing other important areas of life.

- **Distractions** – Arguably, having all employees in the office at the same time each day encourages teamwork and collaboration. But this comes at the cost of distraction, whether that be idle chatter, unnecessary meetings or just general office noise from having a lot of people in a smaller space.

There are a number of alternatives to the 9 to 5, five-days-a-week norm that have been introduced in progressive companies. These companies are willing to shift the culture towards getting the work done, not on clocking a certain number of hours. The shift is not just when you work, but how you work and where you work. Here are a few alternatives:

- **Employees scheduling their own hours** – Employees work as they see best fit – sometimes that means working earlier, sometimes later, sometimes shorter, and sometimes longer. Implementing this requires a high level of trust to get things done and for employees to work responsibly, but if you trust your workforce and your employees are passionate about what they do, the potential benefits are limitless.

- **Less days, but more hours per day** – This won't suit everyone, but some companies and employees have moved to fitting the weekly hours in four, or even three days.

- **Working remotely from the office** – When working from home or another location remote from the office (where the role permits), employees are free from the distractions of the office. And, they can focus on tasks, head down to accomplish more work with more autonomy and flexibility. If they are working remotely from home, the other big benefit is that they can attend to those 5-minute tasks that are required around the home during their breaks, which make a dramatic difference to their lives.

For all the benefits that flexible working brings, none of it can happen without trust. Trust is crucial – to trust employees to take accountability of their own workload and time management to get things done, whether this is at 9 am in the office or 9 pm at home. Trust already exists in every workplace today – employees are trusted with confidential business information. Why not extend this trust to allow some flexibility with work hours?

Case study on working from home

Should more of us be working in our pyjamas some days? Would performance improve if companies encouraged employees to work from home?

To understand the impact of working from home, Ctrip, a NASDAQ listed Chinese travel website company gave the staff at the company's call centre the option to voluntarily work from home for nine months. While half of the volunteers were permitted to telecommute, the rest worked in the office, serving as a control group.

Ctrip expected the employees working from home to be less productive, being away from the discipline of an office environment. However, the results showed the opposite-employees working from home completed 13.5% (or more than half a day per week) more phone calls than office-based staff. Those working from home were also happier, reporting much higher job satisfaction. The number of sick days for employees working from home also dropped dramatically.

The increase in productivity was attributed to two aspects: a quieter working environment, making it easier to process calls; and working more hours-employees were spending some of their normal commute time working and also took shorter breaks.

You may question whether the employees participating in the research knew they were being monitored and measured for productivity. To circumvent this Ctrip conducted the experiment over an extended period of nine months. If employee's activity was influenced by the experiment you would anticipate results to decline over the period of review. However, the positive impact of working from home was constant over that entire period, suggesting that it wasn't driven just by the desire to achieve a good result.

How can technology help us? The pattern of work within the office hasn't changed significantly over many years, even with the increase in technology and connectivity. We work the same number of hours physically in the office and spend even more time in peak hour traffic. But, with 24-hour connectivity, we can be contacted wherever we are. Therefore, it's difficult to place limits on being engaged with work. This overwork can drain our ability to focus.

Think differently; how can technology help rather than hinder productivity?

Clear evidence supports the move away from the 9 to 5 office-based mentality. As you read through the chapters that follow, write notes and visualise how you can increase your output, but with less hours physically at your desk. Or, perhaps working the same hours but at a different start and end time.

Increased output is your greatest weapon to challenge the where and when of your working week. Less hours on the job translates to more hours for leisure. Increased output + more free time = a happy employer and a happy employee. Sounds like a formula we should all strive towards.

Now, let's cover some thought provoking questions and action steps about your work week so that you may get some ideas as to how to gain more time freedom...

? Does the 9 to 5 norm mean you are as productive as you could be, or should you challenge the days and hours to maintain or increase output and improve your life-work integration?

? Do you spend significant time in peak hour traffic? Should you change your working hours in the office to reduce those lost commuting hours?

? How often do you work away from the office or your normal workplace? Would doing this more often assist your output?

1. ☑ Write down what a typical work week looks like for you: what time do you leave home; what time do you arrive at the office; what time do you leave the office; and what time do you get home? What does this look like each day of the week?
2. ☑ Now, start with a blank sheet of paper and design what hours you would work and where you would work during the week to maximise output and hence improve achievement in work and life.
3. ☑ Present your proposed working week to your manager – if it results in the same or greater output, then what has a manager got to challenge?

Now that we have covered the problem with the 40-hour work week and possible solutions, let's discuss how to leverage the power of your own mindset in order to attain life-work balance.

Part 1 – The Power of Your Mindset

"Your beliefs become your thoughts,
Your thoughts become your words,
Your words become your actions,
Your actions become your habits,
Your habits become your values,
Your values become your destiny."
(Mahatma Gandhi)

Desire. Belief. Happiness. Focus. Procrastination. Habits... These topics are all about mindset and will be covered in Part 1. By understanding the impact of your mindset you can improve your life-work relationship starting TODAY.

It all simply starts with a desire, a desire to change, to re-shape the way you spend your time so that you can shine.

When your life is humming along you'll feel better about yourself, and others. The new you will positively impact every single person who comes into contact with you. And you will have a new feeling of confidence and control over your life that you didn't have before.

A powerful desire is where it all starts...

The Power of Desire and Belief

The Power of Desire

> "Desire is the starting point of all achievement, not a hope, not a wish, but a keen pulsating desire which transcends everything." (Napoleon Hill)

Desire is one of the most basic and common human emotions there is. It is as natural as breathing, and normal as the sun rising in the morning. In some religions, desire is a sin and so they do their best to squelch all desire. But even the desire to NOT desire is a desire. It's impossible to stop it.

There are varying degrees of desire, of course. And usually, the more that someone has experienced what they do not want in life, the more powerful their desire is. This is why many multi-millionaires were once completely destitute and broke. When they were down and out, their desire for the opposite was much stronger than normal. The experience of not having enough can help build up a powerful desire.

When it comes to changing anything in your life, you have to have a powerful desire if you're going to make a positive change. You must be clear in your mind as to the cost of continuing with the way things are, versus the positive aspects of a new way.

Do you really have to experience a lot of what you don't want in order to have a powerful desire?

The answer is no.

However, **your desire to change does need to be greater than your desire to stay the same.** And if it's important, you'll find a way. If it isn't, you'll find an EXCUSE.

How can you build up desire so that it is powerful enough?

The secret is knowing your why and ensuring your why is strong enough.

At the heart of your why are your values. For example, if you are a family person, and your highest value is your family, then your "why" is your family. Everything you do, in theory, is related to the wellbeing of your family.

When you are clear about your why and what you want, you pave the way to attain it. When you don't know your why then you set yourself up for others to decide your why for you.

Without a why your desire will wane and probably collapse under pressure, for example, to work overtime rather than get to that exercise class or spend valuable time with friends or family. You are far more likely to be ineffective with your time when you don't have a why.

Your "why" needs to be greater than your "why not". Change is never easy so in order to make change the force for change needs to be greater than the force to not. The choice is yours. Unless you believe you can change; it just won't happen.

If you think you'd like to reduce your excessive work hours but think it's all too hard and you aren't sure what you'll do with your extra leisure time, then chances are your why isn't strong enough and you won't change. On the other hand, for example, if your doctor tells you that you must start exercising in order to deal with a newly diagnosed health problem, then your why to exercise is stronger than your why not – your desire is strong and you'll more than likely make the change to exercise and improve your health.

When others understand your "why," or even just that you have a "why," they are much less likely to impede upon your time outside of work. You would be surprised at how others, including management, will respect your wishes when they know what they are.

But in order to stand up for yourself and your why, you must have a strong belief in yourself...

The Power of Belief

> "If you think you are beaten, you are
> If you think you dare not, you don't,
> If you like to win, but you think you can't
> It is almost certain you won't.
>
> If you think you'll lose, you're lost
> For out of the world we find,
> Success begins with a fellow's will
> It's all in the state of mind.
>
> Life's battles don't always go
> To the stronger or faster man,
> But soon or later the man who wins
> Is the man WHO THINKS HE CAN!"
> (Walter D. Wintle)

What is a belief really?

A belief is a structured set of thought patterns that your subconscious mind has determined is fact, based upon the experiences and events from your past.

The strength of your beliefs is the foundation of performance and success, whether that be at work, on a sporting field, or in any other area of your life.

If you think you are just too busy and this can't feasibly change, it won't.

If you'd like to exercise more but think you don't have the time, it's almost certain you won't.

If you believe you can do something, you're halfway to the finish line; if you believe you can't do it, you aren't even at the starting line.

In the early years of my career, I believed I could achieve at work without working long hours. When child-care became a challenge, I believed I could make it work by working different hours than the typical 9 to 5. My belief shaped my habits and allowed me to achieve the balance I desired.

While training for a half marathon, I lost the belief that I could finish it. As a result, I just couldn't go the distance. When that belief returned, without doing anything else differently, I could suddenly make the distance. Without belief, you just won't get there. With belief, you give yourself every chance possible.

"Whether you think you can, or think you can't, you're right." (Henry Ford)

The self-fulfilling prophecy "believe it and you'll achieve it" is as alive and well today as it was yesterday and will be tomorrow. We are all born with no sense of what we can or can't do. You will never hear a young child say, "I'm not the kind of person who could…"

Our beliefs are acquired one by one along life's journey. During our lives, we limit our horizons through what we learn or are exposed to.

Our subconscious mind creates our strongest beliefs when we are very young. So, for example, if when you were a child, you had to give a speech at school, but it didn't go well, your subconscious mind may have given you the belief that you are a bad public speaker. And if you never challenged that belief, then you could hold on to this belief for the rest of your life.

This type of a negative belief is called a limiting belief. It's powerful and difficult, but very possible to change.

Not all beliefs are limiting beliefs. Just as your subconscious mind can store limiting beliefs, it can also store positive self-beliefs.

The good news is that with time, we can change our beliefs. Just like we learn our limiting beliefs, we can also alter them and learn stronger self-belief.

We need to be aware of our self-beliefs and work towards strengthening our own beliefs. Here are some ideas for increasing your self-belief:

- **Set bold but realistic goals** – The achievement of a goal will build your self-belief. You can then gradually aim higher; and, with each subsequent step forward, you will build your self-belief. Whether you want to lose weight, join a fun run, or climb the corporate ladder, the concept is the same; set a goal that's maybe a bit daring, but realistic enough for you to believe in it.

- **Focus on positive self-talk** – If self-doubt or self-criticism creeps in, challenge it, ignore it or turn up the volume on your positive self-talk to drown it out.

  "If you hear a voice within you say, 'you cannot paint', then by all means paint and that voice will be silenced." (Vincent Van Gogh)

- **Be your own motivational coach** – When you doubt yourself, consider what you would say to someone whom you really believed in if they were having doubts. Sit quietly and say the same things to yourself.

- **Learn to see your accomplishments** – Consciously work on identifying and acknowledging your strengths and achievements, big and small. Spend some time each day thinking about them. This will help you see yourself differently.

- **Continually develop yourself** – Be a life-long learner, and continually aim to better yourself. Self-belief is a reflection of your ability to handle the various aspects of life. The more you grow as a person, the more reasons you have to believe in yourself.

- **Reduce the comparisons between yourself and others** – It's inevitable that no matter how amazing you are, you will always find somebody who is better than you at something. It's human nature to compare but keep your mind busy on other things to reduce the comparison time. Be conscious of when you start to compare and divert your mind elsewhere.

- **Give yourself an unlimited number of opportunities to be successful** – The only true failure is when you give up.

Psychologist Albert Bandura conducted a study that showed the role of attitudes in the presence of failure. Two groups of study participants were required to complete an identical management task. The first group was informed that the purpose of the task involved measuring their management ability. It was explained to the other group that the skills needed to finish the task were simply to be enhanced – that the task was simply an exercise for practicing skills they needed to improve upon. The researchers set up the task in such a difficult fashion that all participants would fail, so of course they all did.

The first group, feeling like failures because their skills weren't adequate, made little or no improvement when given opportunities to repeat the task. The second group, however, perceived each of their failed attempts as a learning opportunity. Oddly enough, they performed at progressively higher levels each time they attempted the task. As far as the second group's perspective of themselves from this experiment, they rated themselves as having more confidence than the first group did.

In other words, your attitude towards a task can make a huge difference on the outcome.

The now-famous individuals listed below started out as your typical brothers, sisters, sons, daughters – people from any neighbourhood. They received their fair share of setbacks, but staying true to their self-belief, they persisted – the results speak for themselves:

- **J.K. Rowling** had all twelve major publishers reject the Harry Potter manuscript. Later the same year, a small publishing house accepted it: Bloomsbury. Today, Rowling's books have sold more than 400 million copies. She is known as the most successful woman author in the United Kingdom.

- **Walt Disney** was fired by an editor due to lack of imagination and having no good ideas. His first company also ended in bankruptcy.

- **Abraham Lincoln** was demoted in the army, had several business failures, and lost eight times when he ran for public office.

- **Thomas Edison** failed to invent the lamp 999 times before he succeeded on the 1000th attempt.

- **Bill Gates**' idea of creating a computer that had a graphic interface and a mouse was rejected when he first submitted these ideas to another company. Stories suggest that the papers detailing the project were thrown in his face.

- **Winston Churchill**, the Nobel Prize-winning, twice-elected prime minister of the United Kingdom struggled in school and failed the sixth grade. After school, he experienced years of political failure, defeated in every election for public office before finally becoming prime minister at the age of sixty-two.

There are so many stories of struggle just before success, and almost every successful person has them. The main point to take home from it is to never give up on your dreams – believe in yourself and keep on trying no matter what obstacles may be in your way.

Belief needs to be maintained throughout any journey because when you stop believing, you could end up quitting right before you were going to become successful.

For most unsuccessful people, they were on the path to success, but then gave up just before they would have made it.

It reminds me of the story of the gold miner in Napoleon Hill's book, "Think and Grow Rich."

The story is set in the gold-rush days when "gold-fever" was common. One man who caught the fever staked his claim and started to dig. Within a few weeks, he hit gold and thought he had struck it rich. Next, he got family and friends to invest in the proper equipment to dig out his gold.

But as he kept digging this one vein of gold, for some odd reason, it suddenly disappeared. He dug everywhere around where the gold vein had stopped and couldn't find it again. Disappointed and distraught, he sold all his gold mining equipment to a junk man and left...

The junk man then hired a mining engineer who said that the first miner didn't know about fault lines. What the junk man and engineer discovered was that the gold was literally only 3 feet away from where the digging had stopped.

The junk man became the millionaire, not the miner who gave up literally 3 feet from his goal...

Just like this miner, most people get very close to becoming a success, and then quit right before they reach their pot of gold.

The moral of the story is to never give up on your belief because you never know just how close you are to breaking through to the sweet rewards of success. You too could be very, very close to success, just don't give up too soon.

In addition to our self-belief, we need to realise that our personal success is also impacted by others around us. Their beliefs about us affect our outcomes.

The Pygmalion effect, or Rosenthal effect, can be defined as the phenomenon whereby higher expectations of any individual will lead to an increase in performance by that person. A corollary of the Pygmalion effect is the Golem effect. This is a phenomenon whereby low expectations of someone lead to a decrease in performance; from a psychological standpoint, both are forms of self-fulfilling prophecy.

> **Our action towards others impacts others beliefs (about us) which causes others actions (towards us) which reinforces our beliefs (about ourselves) which influences our action towards others and the cycle continues.**

The idea behind the Pygmalion effect is this: increasing any leader's expectation of the follower's performance will automatically result in a better performance by that follower. Within the field of sociology, the effect is often cited with regard to education and social class.

Robert Rosenthal and Lenore Jacobson's study of the Pygmalion Effect showed that if teachers were led to expect an enhanced performance from their students, their performances were improved. This study supported the hypothesis that true outcomes, the reality of an individual's efforts, can be positively or negatively influenced directly by the expectations of other people. Rosenthal argued that biased expectancies targeted toward certain subjects could affect reality and create self-fulfilling prophecies regarding those people.

The study involved all students in a single California elementary school being given a disguised IQ test at the beginning of the study. Teachers were not given these scores but were informed that some of their students (about 20 percent of the school, a percentage chosen at random) could be expected to be "intellectual bloomers" that year. These individuals would do better than expected in comparison to their classmates. The bloomers' names were given to the teachers. At the end of the study, a test was given again to all students in the school (the same IQ test used at the beginning of the study). First and second graders showed statistically significant improvements that favoured the experimental group of intellectual bloomers.

This led to the study's conclusion that a teacher's expectations, particularly for the very youngest students, can influence overall student achievement. Rosenthal believed that even attitude or mood could have a definite, positive effect on students, when a specific teacher was made aware of the bloomers. In fact, in times of difficulty, it was concluded that the teacher may pay closer attention to that child, and even treat the child differently. Rosenthal made a prediction that elementary school teachers may subconsciously behave in ways that facilitate the student's success.

The teaching example can also be applied to the workplace. You can put this theory into practice by surrounding yourself with people who have high expectations of you. Their belief in you will subconsciously lift your performance.

In summary, the power of your desire is paramount to your chance of success at anything. One of the most important questions to ask yourself is, "why?" Why do you want what you want? When you are clear as to what your "why" is and when your "why" is big enough, nothing can stop you. Your all important "why" will help you to stay motivated, to stay inspired, and it will carry you through the rough times too. In addition, believing in yourself and your ability to accomplish your goals is also extremely important to the success you will attain. With enough desire and belief in yourself, you can accomplish anything.

? Do you have a strong "why" to change?

? Is your why greater than your why not?

? How strongly do you believe in your life and work goals?

? How can you strengthen your self-beliefs, starting today?

? What do others expect of you? How can you surround yourself with people who have high expectations of you?

1. ☑ Write down what changes you want in life and work. (For example, do you want more time with family and friends? Or do you want more time for a passion project? More time for health, or more time for rest?)

2. ☑ Now, write down why you want to make these changes and what is involved. Note down your why and your why not and challenge whether your desire is strong enough.

3. ☑ And lastly, for this next important question, be honest and write it down. The question is, do you believe you can achieve the change? And who are the people you are going to include in your circle who believe and expect you can make the change?

With enough desire and belief, you can do it!

Your desire, your "why" for wanting to accomplish your goals and your belief are very important. But there is another factor that may be even more important, and that is, your happiness...

Happiness Makes a Huge Difference

"Happiness is not a station you arrive at,
but a manner of travelling."
(Margaret Lee Runbeck)

Take a moment to think about that statement by Margaret Lee Runbeck, "Happiness is not a station you arrive at, but a manner of travelling." There is a lot of wisdom when you analyse it and when you fully understand her statement, it could be a life-changing "aha" moment for you.

What does she really mean?

What she means is that the destination that you are reaching for in life is not really going to bring you the happiness you desire. Rather, it is **the journey to** your destination that will. In other words, the joy is in the journey. You cannot have a happy ending to an unhappy journey. That's not how it works. In other words, you have to find a way to be happy BEFORE you arrive at your destination – before you reach your goal. And once you understand that, you can instantly change your life for the better.

You can choose to be happy at your work regardless of what is going on there. It really is a choice. Never give away your power to anyone nor anything to keep you from being happy. Let that be an inside job that no one can take away from you.

Happiness is not a result. Happiness is a choice, even at work!

There's a clear link between happiness at work, your positivity level, and the productivity and success of you and your team. No system, tool, or methodology can beat the productivity boost you get from your attitude. Your attitude directly impacts your ability to get work done.

The link is obvious, but there is also substantial research proving that happier employees are more productive in the workplace.

A 700-person experiment was conducted in Britain by the Social Market Foundation and the University of Warwick's Centre for Competitive Advantage in the Global Economy. Researchers chose individuals at random, and either showed them a 10-minute comedy clip or provided them with snacks and drinks. They then followed up with a series of questions to ensure that the "happiness shocks," as they're referred to in the report, actually made the subjects happy. When it was confirmed that they did, the researchers gave them tasks to measure their levels of productivity.

The experiment showed that productivity increased by an average of 12% and reached as high as 20% above the control group. Dr Daniel Sgroi, the author of the report, concluded: "Having scientific support for generating happiness-productivity cycles within the workforce should help managers to justify work practices aimed at boosting happiness on productivity grounds."

The Harvard Business Review completed an analysis of hundreds of studies showing the positive benefits of happiness, including, on average: 31% higher productivity; 23% fewer fatigue symptoms; 37% higher sales; three times higher creativity and 10 times more engagement. All very compelling results.

Below is a summary of scientific research findings that support the idea that having a positive attitude makes you more productive. A positive attitude:

- **Enhances your problem-solving skills** – Positive thinking extends your scope of attention, which enhances problem solving. With a negative attitude, you tend to focus on the problem; it becomes difficult to fix, and negativity often multiplies the issue. A positive attitude can turn a bad situation around. When you are happy, you just fix it. Your mind is more open to possibilities, making it easier to solve problems.

  A research study by The National Centre for Biotechnology Information (NCBI) in the United States found that when people were presented with a task, those who had seen a positive video before performing the task did a better job and were more open to solving problems than those who watched an angry or depressing video.

- **Improves decision making** – A positive, happy attitude equals a clearer mind, allowing you to take appropriate action and make more informed decisions – instead of reacting to your emotions.

- **Improves teamwork** – Nothing brings a team together and builds relationships like positivity. Happy, positive people are a lot more pleasurable to be around, have an easier time bonding with others and working in teams, and have better work relationships. This results in greater productivity and success for all.

  People who think positively are more open to trusting others and research studies have also proven that smiling makes it easier for other people to trust you. The more you trust other people, the easier it is to work in a team, because you're open to discussing ideas and building on those ideas collectively.

- **Boosts creativity** – There appears to be a cognitive process that kicks in when we feel good that naturally leads to more flexible, fluent, and original thought processes. There's also a carryover, known as the incubation effect, to the very next day. If an individual is in a good mood on a particular day, they'll be more likely to experience creative ideas that day and the next. This is true for the next day even when a mood change is taken into account (according to a study conducted by Teresa Amabile, Baker Foundation Professor and Director of Research at Harvard Business School).

- **Helps maintain a high energy level** – It's often true that people with a positive attitude have more energy. You'll find that when you think positive thoughts and smile, this results in endorphins being released, which will increase energy. Having more energy means you can accomplish more, increasing your overall productivity.

- **Increases brain stimulation and reduces stress** – People who maintain a positive attitude smile more. In an article posted on TedTalk.com titled, The Hidden Power of Smiling, Ron Gutman reveals how studies have found that smiling is known to increase brain activity. The more positive thoughts you experience, and the more you smile, the better your brain will function.

Here's another benefit: It's been proven that smiling reduces stress. Stress clouds your mind and will certainly weigh you down, whereas focusing on thinking positive thoughts and smiling a lot reduces stress. The result of this is that you'll find it's easier to focus and get things done.

Does being productive automatically make us happy, or does being happy play a role in our productivity? It works either way, but studies have shown the correlation is most powerful when starting with happiness (thinking in a positive way and smiling on purpose) translating into productivity. This means that if you want to be more productive, the best approach is to focus on being happy as you perform your tasks and strive to reach your goals.

What can you do in order to be happier? Here are some happiness habits. How many are you practicing today?

- Show kindness to other people
- Forgive often
- Appreciate more
- Live in the present
- Practise acceptance
- Exercise
- Dream big
- Make time to play

- Take time to recharge
- Give yourself a treat
- Congratulate yourself
- Care for yourself
- Smile and laugh whenever possible

It's important to be happy at work and at home too. Not many people who are miserable at home and happy at work end up being great team members. The best team members that normally surface in any organisation, whether they're at a cash register, unloading a truck, or in the management team in the office have great home and work integration. This is why it's so important to have fun and enjoy all of life, all hours of the day.

A lot of us get trapped into the belief that we aren't going to be happy until something outside of ourselves makes us happy. For example, we think that we can't be happy until we get our dream house, or our dream car, or that perfect relationship.

But that is living a very conditional life where we depend upon conditions outside of ourselves in order to be happy. And when you live a conditional life like that, you give your power away to outside conditions. A lot of us give our power away to other people, circumstances and events when we depend upon outside conditions to make us happy.

The result? If conditions don't change, we never become happy.

What can you do in order to be happy first, without being dependent upon conditions?

The answer is realise that happiness is an inside job. It's the first job. It's the main job. And when you become happy first for no good reason, then you will become unstoppable because nothing can bring you down – no thing and no-one will then have control over your emotions – only YOU will be in control.

There is the story of Viktor Frankl, the psychologist who was stuck in a Nazi concentration camp during World War II to illustrate this point.

One day, he and the others were given just the head of a fish in a bowl of water as their meal for the day. But rather than think of how horrible his situation was, how hungry he was, and how there was no meat from the fish to eat, Viktor appreciated what was given to him and he even found beauty in the head of the fish.

In other words, he found a way to be thankful and happy in the most deplorable conditions imaginable. Because of his positive attitude, he believes, Dr. Frankl lived to tell his story.

The question becomes, if Dr. Frankl could find the feeling of appreciation and happiness while in a concentration camp, given whatever situation you are now in, can you find those feelings too? Can you find reasons to appreciate no matter how bad your situation is?

When you can be happy no matter what is going on in your life, you have won – you have mastered the secret of life.

The good news is more and more employers understand that an unhappy employee is an unproductive employee. And that the best employees are the ones who are the happiest at home and work.

Embrace "Good Stress"

It's difficult to be productive when you're stressed out. It's hard to stay focused when you're thinking about deadlines, problems, or an overwhelming amount of work that needs to be done in what never seems to be enough time.

Stress is a physiological response to a change in our environment and is designed primarily to keep us safe. It's well documented that stress is at the root of many modern-day ailments, and the workplace remains a key cause of stress. Stress is seen as the primary culprit for all feelings of discomfort and dismay, and to be avoided at all costs. However, whether we like it or not, stress is an unavoidable fact of life.

However, stress, whilst managed, can have the following positives impacts:

- **Learning and development-**One of the recent theories regarding stress provides this argument: we basically have stress, not for survival in the immediate sense, but because we wouldn't have the opportunity to learn from the stressful situation without the stress it brings. Early man may have had a stressful reaction so he could escape a tiger but feeling this kind of pressure is not a healthy way to respond to our lives today. We all need to understand that stress triggers all sorts of mechanisms biologically, and we can learn how to grow and develop psychologically from the pressure. How we react to stress, those times when our heart is pounding, is key to keeping ourselves mentally and physically healthier.

  Psychologists say it's not the amount of stress or the severity of it that will harm us. It is actually our belief in whether or not that stress will cause us to sustain harm that matters – the power of our belief!

Rather than believe that stress is toxic, perhaps the key is unlocking what we believe about stress and finding ways to embrace it and use it for good in our lives. If each of us can comprehend that stress has the ability to enhance our performance in life and assist us in personal growth, then it will accomplish that in our lives. We can think of it as a gift, if it's managed properly.

- **Improved immunity-**Research tells us that short-term stress can actually improve our immunity. As the body responds to stress at a given time, it is actually preparing one's system for the possibility of some type of infection or injury. A Stanford study conducted in 2012 concluded that lab rats had a clear reaction to mild stress. The rats had a "massive mobilisation" of several different types of immune cells in their blood upon subjection to stress.

- **Resilience-**Interestingly enough, stress can cause you to become more resilient. When you learn to deal with all types of stressful situations, this can help you deal more easily with stressful situations in the future. This conclusion was reached in a body of research conducted to examine the science of resilience.

- **Motivation-**Stress can also motivate you to succeed. Good stress may be just the thing you need to get a task completed at your workplace. Consider an impending deadline. Stress can influence your behaviour in a positive way; it can prompt you to manage a situation productively and rapidly. The key is to look at stressful situations as attainable challenges. Tell yourself you can meet it head on, rather than perceiving it as being too overwhelming, an unpassable roadblock.

If you expect to experience stress and fully recognise that you have the natural ability to thrive under pressure, you will be healthier than if you try to avoid all stress by fearing it or suppressing it. Studies show that people who see their racing heart or sweaty palms as a signal that they are receiving energy from the body will actually do better under the stress. They rise to the occasion by performing better than they normally would. In this frame of mind, they make better decisions and end up impressing others with their overall performance in the stressful situation.

There are many ways to approach stress management. The most commonly perceived method is to learn to thrive under pressure, to embrace (and even love) deadlines. It helps to enjoy competition – making up your mind that you always want to push yourself. This type of behaviour and attitude exemplifies the Iron Man model of stress.

However, this approach is just one way of managing stress well. Even if you're not really the type of person who thrives under pressure, and you don't enjoy being competitive, this doesn't mean that you can't learn to be good at handling stress. You may thrive in stressful circumstances in a different way. For instance, you might do this through connection and compassion, not through a sense of competition or feeling aggression. You might have the ability to use stress as a catalyst for connecting with other people – through having compassion, experiencing empathy, and feeling more connection, thereby strengthening your relationships.

Another way of being good at stress involves giving it some type of meaning. This might come from appreciating yourself more and by recognising your strengths, plus appreciating help provided for stressful situations from your community. You might say, "This is going to do something positive for me and other people, so the stress is worth it." Or, you might tell yourself, "Even though I am terrified right now, this experience has helped me cultivate courage." You might also have the ability to look back at a stressful situation and say, "Well, even though this stress was horrible and I wish it hadn't happened, I can take it as a learning experience that gave me knowledge of XYZ." You can deal well with stress by having a philosophical approach, even if you don't run on adrenaline surges or cope by isolating yourself from others during stress.

To manage all aspects of your stress levels and separate good from bad symptoms, keep a positive attitude. Remain calm, even in the face of chaos; assess your options, then decide on the next steps to take; lead others by example; and stay off the drama train. Keep things in perspective, too. Ask yourself this question: What is the very worst thing that could happen, and what is the chance that it actually could happen?

The bottom line is that when you view stress as a good thing, then that is what it will become. Your beliefs are that powerful.

?   Do you generally have a positive or negative attitude at work? Are you aware of how this impacts your productivity?

?   What can you start or stop doing today to make your days happier and allow you to get through your day more effectively?

?   How did you react to stress today?

?   Do you recognise your triggers for stress?

?   How can you embrace stress?

1. Review the list of happiness habits listed in this chapter and note down which ones you aren't practising today. How can you consciously exercise some of these ideas? For a while they will be rituals, it will take time doing them repeatedly for them to become habits.
2. Tell others around you what you are up to and ask for their feedback on whether they can see a change in you.
3. After a number of weeks take time out to answer the question of whether creating these habits is making you feel happier and, hence increasing your productivity.

4. ☺ Think about how you believe you manage stress and ask your peers, manager, team, family and/or friends how they think you react to stress.
5. ☑ Document how you can think differently about stress in order for it to help rather than hinder you.

Your attitude can make a huge difference in how happy you are, and in how productive you are. Even having a positive attitude about stress can greatly increase your ability to handle it well. And now that you are more aware of these truths, what other things can you do in order to be more successful, productive and happy?

How to Focus and Stop Procrastinating

"The person who tries to do everything ultimately achieves nothing. Focus proceeds greatness." (Robin Sharma)

The ability to focus on what really matters, efficiently and effectively, is an essential attribute for success. We live in an age of distraction; yet one of life's paradoxes is that our brightest future hinges on our ability to pay attention to the present. We need to starve distractions that work to pull us away from the task at hand and feed our focus.

By focusing all your attention on just one thing, you can give it the attention it needs, and you will get results.

Social media, along with other types of digital distractions, don't interrupt us if we close out of them and learn to focus ourselves fully on the task before us. If we need to spend time on email or text others, we can put aside everything else and just be fully focused on that single digital task.

If your job demands that you totally focus on a task defined as urgent, you may stress out because you have a million other things to do. Your time is very limited, and you don't have time to do everything. Or, you can choose to be present, focusing fully on that task. And now, there is only that one task before you. When you're done, you can simply move forward to the next task.

We need not only to focus, but also to fix that focus and narrow it like a laser to an attention span that remains constant and unwavering – in order to immerse ourselves completely in the task. Immersing oneself completely in a task is called flow.

Flow can be defined as the mental state one operates in that causes a person to perform an activity fully engaged with a feeling of being energised. This means the individual has energised focus. He or she is completely involved with the work or activity at hand, enjoying the process of it all. The essence of this is characterised by complete absorption in the activity, during which a person feels the flow and doesn't notice much else. Mihály Csíkszentmihályi has named this state of achieving flow in colloquial terms as "being in the zone."

Being present, being in the zone, is a good option for managing any problem. It's a way to more easily handle any problem, any distraction, or stressful situation at hand. This focus on your part allows everything else to fade away, leaving only you and any tasks you're dealing with right now.

Focusing on the present has a lot of great benefits. It allows you to stay calmer in a stressful environment or situation. It allows you to put limits on time spent allowing your mind to wander, from thinking about the past and regrets to dwelling on the future and feeling anxious about situations that haven't even occurred yet. Focus permits concentration on the one area you can truly control: the present. Focusing on the present increases your productivity and your effectiveness overall.

Concentrating on the now, rather than the past or the future, isn't easy though; it takes some practice. If you practice being present on a regular basis, similar to other tasks, you become increasingly proficient at it. It eventually becomes a mode of being, not just a task on your list.

Most people don't learn to be fully present. This isn't because it's hard to do, but due to the fact that they don't practice. Practice, more practice, and being present will become natural, it will become a habit. Here are some ways to practice focusing on the present:

- **When you eat, just eat**. Pay attention to what you're eating and do it slowly. The same applies to other activities such as driving and washing dishes. Don't try to do multiple things at once – just do what you're doing now, and nothing else.

- **Become more aware of your thoughts**. Most likely, you will think about the past and future – that's okay. Awareness will bring change. Spend time just thinking about the present.

- **Try meditation**. Meditation is a practice that lets an individual train the mind or induce a different mode of consciousness, either to realise some benefit or for the mind to simply acknowledge its content without becoming identified with that content. Anything that quiets your racing thoughts can be your form of meditation: exercise, a repetitive task like washing dishes, or a soak in the bath, as examples.

How to Meditate

Studies show that all of us have about 60,000 thoughts every day and most of those thoughts are not positive. However, the act of meditating will help you to calm your mind and body down, distil the negative thoughts, resulting in the ability to focus better. It has many other health benefits too.

You may think that you don't have time to meditate, but studies show that in reality, meditation will help you to be more productive and efficient for the entire rest of the day. That's why it's recommended. If your "why" is big enough, you'll find the time.

The best time to meditate is in the morning. All you will need is a comfortable place to sit, a timer, perhaps an eye mask and about 10 to 20 minutes. And before you get started, ensure you aren't hungry or that you don't need to use the restroom.

Dim the room you are in and set the timer for 10 to 20 minutes (20 minutes is ideal but as a beginner 10 minutes is a great start). Next, close your eyes, take a deep breath in, hold it for about 3 seconds, and let it out slowly to the count of about 6 seconds. Repeat that 3 times. The reason why this is important is that when you breathe out slowly for over 6 seconds on the out-breath, your subconscious mind gets the signal that you are safe to relax. Now, keep focusing on your breathing and relax. The idea is to keep yourself from thinking any thoughts while you are in a state of awareness. When a thought does come in, just let it go – let it go by like as if it was a float in a parade. After 10 to 20 minutes, you're done!

The worst thing you can do while meditating is to worry that you're not doing it right. After doing it for 28 days or so, it will become a habit that you may learn to truly enjoy.

How to Stop Procrastination

> "This constant, unproductive preoccupation with all the things we have to do is the single largest consumer of time and energy." (Kerry Gleeson)

Procrastination makes easy things hard and hard things harder. Imagine all the things you'd accomplish if you never procrastinated.

You are who you are because of either motivation or procrastination. By allowing yourself to put things off, you are likely dealing with an impact that can have greater implications than you realise. To begin with, it fosters distress.

Besides the presence of stress and guilt that are connected to procrastination, consider the other consequences of putting off what you need to do, such as earning a bad reputation with colleagues, friends, and family – and losing your ambition to succeed and failing to accomplish your dreams.

You procrastinate when you ignore and delay tasks that you should be concentrating on at the moment. This is usually done in favour of taking on something that brings more enjoyment, or an activity or task that you're more comfortable doing. According to psychologist Professor Clarry Lay, a prominent writer on this particular subject, procrastination occurs when there's "a temporal gap between intended behaviour and enacted behaviour." The bottom line is that procrastination involves a significant amount of time between when people intend to do a job, and when they get around to actually doing it.

Procrastination is common, yet you may not even realise you are doing it. When you unknowingly avoid performing a task, you create various reasons in your mind for delaying that given task at hand – sometimes indefinitely. To stop this type of avoidance behaviour, you have to recognise it as procrastination. Facing the facts is half the battle in stopping this approach to work and life. Here are some indicators to help you identify times when you're procrastinating:

- Your daily schedule is full of low-priority tasks from your to-do list.

- You read e-mails several times, without answering or deleting them – or even deciding what you want to do with them.

- You sit down to focus on a task you'd classify as high priority, but almost immediately get up to make yourself a cup of coffee.

- A specific item is still on your to-do list after a long period of time, even though you know it's important.

- You regularly agree to those unimportant tasks other people are asking you to do, spending your time on them instead of moving forward with important items already on your list.

- You wait until you're in the "right mood" or it's the "right time" to tackle an important job. You may tell yourself you need a specific amount of time, physical space, equipment, or whatever, then wait for everything to come together magically. Oddly enough, the magic rarely shows up!

Procrastination is an ingrained habit, so you can't break it overnight. Bad habits only come under your control when you have persistently stopped practicing them. So, use as many approaches as possible to maximise your chances of defeating them.

As Sir Isaac Newton taught us a very long time ago, objects at rest tend to remain at rest and objects in motion tend to stay in motion. This applies to humans just as well as it does to falling apples. Here are some general tips to get you going and keep you moving:

- **If the task takes less than two minutes**, do it now.

- **If the job seems overwhelming, break the project up** into a set of smaller, more manageable tasks. Break it down into little parts, then focus on one part at a time. If you still procrastinate on the task after breaking it down, break it down even further.

- **Begin with some quick, small tasks** if you can, even if logically these don't seem like the initial actions to take. By just starting something, you'll feel that you're achieving things – so perhaps the whole project won't seem so overwhelming after all.

- **Make a smart to-do list** by writing down only the tasks that you're avoiding, not the ones you know you'll do anyway. Then back this up by defining deadlines.

- **Identify the unpleasant consequences** of not completing the task. Come up with a consequence that will deter you from putting it off.

- **Stop waiting for the perfect time**; there's never a perfect time. Think of a task/project you undertook and performed perfectly with no mistakes at all. Hard to think of something? If you keep waiting for one, you're never going to accomplish anything. Perfectionism is one of the biggest reasons for procrastination. No matter how inexperienced, uneducated, or unprepared you might feel, right now is the best time to jump into action.

- **Make your intentions public**. It's a great way to keep yourself accountable to your plans. This will add pressure. For some of us, avoiding embarrassment is the mightiest motivator.

- **Set a time to complete a task**, so that you have no time for procrastination.

- **Reward yourself for finishing the task**.

- And lastly, **Act. Do it! Get on with it.** You can strategise, plan and hypothesise all day – but if you don't take action, nothing will happen.

The longer you can avoid procrastination, the greater your chances of stopping this negative habit for good will be! The best way to get something done is to begin.

? Are you conscious of when you need to focus, but you're just not getting into the flow?

? What is stopping you from focusing – is it the environment, a digital device, your energy level or combination of challenge and skill?

? How can you practice being present?

? Are you aware when you are procrastinating?

? What tips can you use to minimise procrastination?

? What price will you pay if you fail to accomplish delayed tasks versus enjoying the feeling of reaching specific goals you've been putting off?

Focus

1. ☑ If you are not aware of how well you focus, then for this next week, keep a journal of how well you focus. A suggestion is provided in the Managing Your Energy Levels chapter of how to track your focus as well as other measures.

2. ☑ Once aware of your focus opportunities, note these down including what needs to change in order for you to focus – is it your office environment? Or is it your connectivity, phone, email distractions – what is it?

3. ☑ Develop an action plan for focus improvement including how do you form new habits.
4. ☑ Follow your plan day after day, night after night, until the positive changes become a habit.

Procrastination

1. ☑ If procrastination is a problem for you, put the words "Stop Procrastinating!" in a visible place, perhaps at the top of your computer screen.
2. 💬 Share your procrastination challenges with a work colleague, friend or family member and talk through how they can become an accountability partner and help you become accountable for change.
3. ✖ Each time you recognise yourself procrastinating, as hard as it may seem, just stop procrastinating. Take at least some action. Remember, no change is easy, but you'll be rewarded with the outcome!

In order to focus and stop procrastinating, you really need to learn how to make it a habit – the topic of the next chapter.

The Secret to Developing Good Habits

"There is no influence like the influence of habit." (Gilbert Parker)

This is one of the most important chapters in the whole book for you to put into practice...

Everything that is covered in this book will only be successful if it's made into a habit – whether that be how you focus, how you prioritise, how you manage your inbox, how you start or end your day, or how you manage your energy levels. Habits are crucial if you want to attain healthy life-work balance and integration.

Today, your life is essentially comprised of the sum of all your habits. When you woke up this morning, you probably did multiple routine habits in the same order as yesterday. What did you do first today? Did you have a coffee, check your phone, and then have a shower? Did you brush your teeth before or after the shower? Which shoe did you put on first and which shoelace (if you have shoelaces) did you tie first? What did you say to others in your home? If you did most of these actions in the same order as yesterday and the day before, then they have become a habit. Most of the choices you make each day may appear to be decisions you are making but they aren't – they are in fact, habits.

You first make your habits, and then your habits make you. For example, how in shape or out of shape you are is directly the result of your habits. Not only that, but your habits determine how happy or unhappy you are. Habits directly impact how successful or unsuccessful you are. What you repeatedly do on a consistent basis (for instance, dwell on certain thoughts or participate in certain activities) will ultimately shape who you are as a person, and the type of personality you display.

How productive you are in life does not depend on discipline in isolation; rather, it also depends on making sure you form good habits. Of course, none of us are so mechanically disciplined that we automatically do all the right things all the time. But it's true that the most successful people are those who have formed good habits. These individuals aren't necessarily more intelligent or disciplined than the general population. The common denominator of those who are successful has proven to be their habits. They've invested the time to form good habits; they've devoted their time to doing the right things on a consistent basis.

If you want to achieve and maintain discipline over time, then select aspects of your life that you want to apply good habits to consistently; they may be tasks you consider mundane, even boring. The secret is to "routinise" these areas of your life so you can address them without spending a lot of time; they will happen subconsciously. The result is the need to make fewer decisions by figuring out ahead of time how you will make these things happen.

Habit Formation

There are three phases of habit formation:
1.   Making an activity a ritual
2.   Turning that ritual into a routine
3.   Exercising that routine until it is a habit

Motivation will get you started; a habit will keep you going. A ritual requires conscious effort, both for remembering to do it at all and doing it correctly. A habit just happens.

Here are some tips for creating a ritual, turning that ritual into a routine, and exercising that routine until it is a habit:

•   **Be clear on the why** – In the words of the German philosopher, **Friedrich Nietzsche, "If you know the why, you can live anyhow"**. In other words, when you identify a deep significance to any habit you want to acquire or goal you wish to achieve, this will encourage you to overcome the stubborn obstacles and inevitable frustrations that will get in your way.

•   **Write down your reasons** – Writing down the reasons you want to form the habit or reach the goal can be very helpful. This makes your ideas clearer and helps you focus on your desired result, as well as giving you a greater sense of their reality.

•   **Start with simple tweaks** – Forget trying to completely redo your life in one day. Resist the temptation to become overly motivated and plan too many changes at once. In the words of **Leo Babauta, "Make it so easy, you can't say no."**

- **The two-minute rule** is geared toward the idea that by simply getting started, you can make all sorts of good things happen. These ideas can inspire you:

  o   Want to eat healthier? Just eat one piece of fruit, and you'll often find yourself inspired to make a healthy salad as well.

  o   Want to make reading a habit? Just read the first page of a new book, and before you know it, the first three chapters have flown by.

  o   Want to train for a half marathon? Just get your running shoes on and get out the door, and you'll end up putting kilometres on your legs.

- **Make it daily** – Lasting change is a consequence of daily habits, not a magical transformation. If you want to make a habit stick, remember that consistency is critical. For instance, if you want to change a bad habit of checking your emails on your phone each night before bed, don't think "I'll just stop on a Tuesday and Wednesday and check the other nights" – the change needs to be consistent across all nights and for about twenty-eight days in order to form a good habit.

  The same applies if you want to begin an exercise program – start going to the gym each day for the first twenty-eight days or so. Going only a couple of times a week makes it more difficult to create a habit. Activities you participate in once every few days are much trickier to keep up, making it next to impossible to break a bad habit, or form a good habit.

- **Be consistent** – The more consistently you practice a given habit, the easier it'll be to keep it up. If you want to start exercising, try going to the same place at the same time every day. If you want to form the habit of waking up earlier, set your alarm clock for the same time every morning. When mental cues like having a specific time of day, place, and circumstances are identical from day to day, it's easier to make a habit stick.

- **Record your progress** – Write your habit clearly on your calendar, so you can envision your progress with ease (seeing your progress feels good, encouraging you to take positive forward steps).

- **Associate with positive role models** – Spend more time with those individuals who exemplify the habits you want to mirror. Remember that you become very similar to what you spend time around.

- **Set a reminder** – This productive reminder to encourage yourself doesn't depend on feeling motivated, and it won't require you to necessarily remember a new habit. A good reminder makes it easy for you to start by encoding your new behaviour into something you already do. You could, for example, take a walk around the school track while you're waiting for your child to get out of school each afternoon. Setting up a highly visible reminder – such as putting your keys where you can't help but see your walking shoes, reminding you to take them with you and put them on as soon as you're on school grounds – links a new habit (walking) with a current behaviour (picking up your child). This makes it much easier to change.

- **Commit to one to two months** – You may have read that it takes twenty-eight days to make a habit; however, according to a number of studies, the time it takes to form a habit really isn't that clear-cut. Researchers from University College London examined the new habits of ninety-six people over the space of twelve months and found that the average time it took for a new habit to stick was sixty-six days. Individual times ranged from eighteen to 254 days. If you want to develop a new behaviour, it will take time. You shouldn't give up if three weeks doesn't do the trick. Stick with it.

- **Reward yourself; celebrate success** – We all desire to continue doing those things that make us feel good. That's why it's important to reward yourself along the way. It's true that an action needs to be repeated to become a habit, so deliberately decide to reward yourself for successfully practicing your habit – every time, if possible.

A Great Example of the Power of Habits and Morning Routine - Well-known author John Grisham started writing his first book in 1984. At the time, he led a busy life; he worked as a lawyer full time and had a young family. Despite his time constraints, he had a strong belief in himself, in the power of his idea to see it through. He made the choice to fit writing a book into his life.

When he first started writing, Grisham had "these little rituals that were silly and brutal, but very important." He said, "The alarm clock would go off at five, and I'd jump in the shower. My office was five minutes away. And I had to be at my desk, at my office, with the first cup of coffee, a legal pad and write the first word at 5.30, five days a week. I was very disciplined about it."

His goal was to write a page every day. Sometimes that would take ten minutes, sometimes an hour; often, he would write for two hours before he had to turn to his job as a lawyer.

It took John a total of three years to finish his first novel, A Time to Kill. However, his method of working paid off tremendously. Since he got his first book published in 1988, Grisham has continually written one book per year. To date, he has sold more than 300 million copies worldwide. This all started with one page per day. That one positive habit done daily was the basis for changing his life.

Grisham's habits are strong; he still writes at the same place, same table, same chair, with the same cup and type of coffee each day. There are examples like this everywhere. How can you make a new habit into a future success story for yourself?

Tools and techniques relating to productivity and increased output can become habits – so they just happen without any conscious thought.

You could make it a habit each evening before you leave your workplace to identify the most important priorities for the next day.

You could make it a habit that those most important tasks are your very first priority when you get into your workplace the next morning.

You could make it a habit to get your gym gear out the night before a morning session so that when you get out of bed you are ready to go.

You could make it a habit to only check your emails certain times of the day.

Or you could make it a habit to leave the office by x time each day and it will just happen.

You can apply a habit lens to a large percentage of your life, both at work and at home. You will be amazed at the positive impact it can have on your life.

?   Are there habits you've wanted to form, but to date you haven't succeeded? Why is that?

?   What steps do you need to take to make some of your rituals into habits?

?   What productivity techniques should you turn into habits? Can you start taking action today?

1. ☑ Write down 1-3 bad habits that you want to eliminate and write down 1-3 good habits you'd like to form – make at least one of these habits life related and one work related.
2. ☑ For each habit, write down your why – what's the significance of the bad habit you want to break or good habit you want to form? How will the habit formation/change impact your everyday?
3. ☑ Prioritise your habits based on how strong your why is. On the basis of it taking at least 28 days to form/change a habit, you now have a plan for a number of months to come.
4. ☑ Take your highest priority habit and write down your plan:
   a. What simple tweaks can you start with to get you going?
   b. What are you going to do to ensure you are consistently making the change daily?

    c.   What does progress look like and how are you going to record your progress?

5.   💬 Find an accountability partner – they could be a work colleague, friend, family member, neighbour and tell them what change(s) you want to make. Agree with them how often you want to check-in and how they can help make your change successful.

6.   🎉 Celebrate success!

Now that we have covered mindset, let's get into the more practical information which is going to help you to start your day well, prioritise tasks, and manage your energy levels.

Part 2 – How to Structure Your Day

This next part is more about the practical application of balancing life and work. You're going to learn about why starting your day well begins the night before, how to prioritise your day, how to manage your energy, why eating dinner with your family every night is so important and more.

This part is all about how to organise your day so that you maximise your productivity.

It's practical. It's scientific. And it works.

But like everything else, you have to work on these things in order to make it into a habit. And once you make it a habit, it will be easy, it will become second nature.

So, let's start with how to start your day.

Starting Your Day Well

"Every day think as you wake up-today I am fortunate to have woken up, I am alive, I have a precious human life, and I am not going to waste it. I am going to use all my energies to develop myself, to expand my heart out to others, to achieve enlighten-ment for the benefit of all beings, I am go-ing to have kind thoughts towards others, I am not going to get angry or think badly about others, I am going to benefit others as much as I can." (Dalai Lama)

Quiet time in the morning is precious – that time before the outside world bleeds noise into your day. For most of us, mornings set the tone for the rest of the day. Establishing an effective morning routine sets the foundation for happiness, high energy and achievement throughout the workday.

Unfortunately, an average morning for many people doesn't start as the Dalai Lama suggests. For many, it involves hitting the snooze button multiple times, feeling incredibly time pressured, getting frustrated with others in the household, rushing out the door with little to no breakfast and arriving in the office feeling exhausted before the day even begins. Much like this scenario, is the start of your day less than ideal?

It's challenging to perform at a high level and make a significant contribution on any given day if the start of your day is stressful. The rushed, uninspired behaviour can contribute to a negative, unproductive attitude for the remainder of the day. But making some simple changes in your morning routine can transform a specific area of your life more quickly than you would ever think possible.

Benefits of a productive morning routine:

- **Structure and success** – One of the positive outcomes of healthy morning rituals is that you start your day with structure. This planned routine for each morning gives you direction. Morning routines that work well for you also have a positive result at the end of the day: early structure in your day allows you to enjoy some lack of structure towards the end of the day. Following a productive routine with planned discipline and accomplishing everything you've set out to do in the earlier hours of the morning sets you up to relax and unwind later.

- **Mental advantages** – Reflect for a moment: How different would your life be if you were consistently in a better frame of mind and had a happier disposition? According to a study by the American Psychological Association, many of us can experience great results by creating and following a better morning routine. Our stress, depression, and anxiety levels will start to decline – and our life satisfaction levels will escalate, even soar. The study reported that healthy changes caused participants to feel more motivated, and their to-do lists seemed less daunting.

- **Physical benefits** – Productive morning routines lead to improved physical benefits, as well. A harmonious beginning to your day will help you feel more energetic and stronger. Additionally, when you use the morning time after you first wake up to engage in some form of exercise – a cardio workout, yoga session, or a morning walk – you'll also experience better health.

- **More quality time** – In today's world, all of us are faced with many different demands on our time. The feeling many of us have is that we are neglecting ourselves. We say, "I never have time for me!" By changing your morning routine to have a positive impact on your life, you'll discover this results in, unintentionally, creating time for yourself – so you can focus on your own needs and desires.

To improve your morning routine, try the following suggestions:

- **Stop telling yourself you aren't a morning person** – You may think that because you have never been a morning person that it's just not possible to change. However, you can change your underlying beliefs and gear your mindset toward making a productive morning routine a daily habit. The key lies in your mind. By deciding to overcome the invisible script of "I'm not a morning person" that you've believed for so long, you set yourself up for newfound success. According to author Ramit Sethi, invisible scripts are assumptions that are so much a part of your world view and choices that you don't question them at all. Often, there's an inner voice telling you what you should, need to, or can't do. So, if you keep telling yourself that you're not a morning person, your mind makes sure your belief is true.

- **Eat a healthy breakfast** – It's crucial to enjoy a healthy breakfast. It's considered the most important meal of the day because it ends the overnight fasting state. Breakfast will replenish your blood sugar level by supplying glucose, which will instantly accelerate your metabolism. It also provides key nutrients essential for the energy you need to accomplish all the things you need to do. Many studies have linked eating breakfast to good health – including better memory and concentration, both needed to be productive.

- **Stop hitting the snooze button** – Comedian Demitri Martin summed up the insanity of snoozing perfectly when he said: "Hitting the snooze button in the morning doesn't even make sense... It's like saying 'I hate getting up in the morning, so I do it over and over and over again.'"

  The science behind why the snooze button is bad for you is this: throughout the night, we experience cycles of both deep sleep and light sleep. Each cycle lasts about ninety to one hundred minutes. Deep sleep, which is more difficult to wake up from, occurs early on and dominates after falling sleep; light sleep occurs closer to one's natural waking time. It's much easier to be woken from light sleep.

  It's apparent how our body rhythms could be affected by the snooze button. Each time we fall asleep, or fall back asleep, our sleep cycle starts over at the beginning. It's natural that shortly before waking, each of us should experience lighter sleep. If we were to sleep with no alarm clock, these factors would naturally allow our bodies to gradually adjust and prepare for waking.

Using an alarm clock means that we may wake in the middle of a sleep cycle, meaning our bodies haven't had time to prepare. This can easily cause an increase in sleep inertia, which most of us are very familiar with – that groggy feeling immediately upon waking. This tempts us to hit the snooze button so we can fall back asleep.

However, when you press the snooze button and most likely fall back asleep, this sets you up for more stress. Your sleep cycle will start over from the beginning – except this time, when your alarm goes off, you're in a deeper stage of sleep. You'll have a much harder time of waking up. The result of this new cycle is that the last portion of your sleep will become very fragmented and out of rhythm. This means you will miss out on the recovery benefits of consolidated sleep. Your ability to function effectively for the remainder of the day may be very impaired.

The best way to resist using the snooze button is to discipline yourself to create a regular sleep schedule, every day of the week. Define your exact bedtime and waking time and stick to it, even on weekends. Your body will adjust naturally after a while, and you'll find that it will be easier to wake up every morning.

The best morning routines begin the night before

If you want to wake up and literally bounce out of bed with enthusiasm, then you'll want to make sure you end the previous day in the best way possible.

Be sure to compile tomorrow's to-do list at the end of the day today. By sorting out tomorrow's top priorities before today ends, your mind can focus on the important things to be done before you go to your job and begin work.

Also, be sure to decide what clothes you'll be wearing the following day; you'll save precious time in the morning. Otherwise, you'll be standing at your wardrobe just gazing at the clothes hanging in front of you wasting precious time. To save even more time, why not select your exercise clothes too, so you can quickly put them on in the morning? Choosing these clothes, the night before will encourage you to stick with your morning exercise habit!

?   Is your morning routine providing you every opportunity to perform well throughout the day?

?   Are you addicted to the snooze button?

?   How can you improve your morning routine?

?   Are you planning your day ahead the evening before?

1.   ☑ Be honest with yourself – how good is your morning routine? Write down what you would or should change with your morning routine.
2.   ☑ Repeat point 1 for your night routine.
3.   🎤 Develop a plan of how you can make a positive change and be realistic.
4.   ◎ Follow your plan day after day, night after night, until the positive changes become a habit, and it will just happen!

Now that you have your day off to a good start, how do you decide what task to do first?

Prioritising Your Most Important Tasks

"The key is not to prioritise what's on your schedule, but to schedule your priorities"
(Stephen Covey)

Do you know what your most important tasks are? And do they take priority each day? Congratulations if you answered yes to both of these questions. Unfortunately for most of us, that's not the case. Most of the time, we are not clear on what our most important tasks are, or perhaps it's that we just don't give them the attention they deserve. Usually the small, unimportant tasks that need to get done every day get in the way of important tasks.

To illustrate how to prioritise tasks, Mark Twain gave us some advice:

> **"If it's your job to eat a frog, it's best to do it first thing in the morning. And if it's your job to eat two frogs, it's best to eat the biggest one first."**

In other words, your "frog" is the task that will have the greatest positive impact on your outcomes at that point in time. Your frog is your **"Most Important Task" (MIT)**. If you have two frogs, for example, two tasks, then just like with the biggest frog, start with the biggest, hardest, and most important task first.

The idea is that no matter what else is going on in the day, the MITs are what you want to be sure of doing.

You may be wondering why do the MITs first. Most of us are at our cognitive best, our brain at optimal performance, about two to four hours after we've woken up, regardless of whether we think we are a morning or night person. Yet, we often waste that time on easy, relatively unimportant tasks like emails, or that morning coffee run which could be postponed to later in the day. It makes most sense to do the MITs when we are our cognitive best.

And unless you intentionally schedule time for certain work, MITs included, you tend not to get to it. In order to improve this situation, each night, make it a habit to identify the MIT(s) for the next day. And make this your very first priority the next morning.

How to find your MITs:

1. Write down everything on your to-do list, both business as usual and project-related tasks.
2. Ask yourself: If I could only do one thing all day (and you want it to be the task that will have the greatest effect on your role), what task would I choose?
3. Move that task to your MIT list.
4. Replicate this for a second and, if needed, third MIT.

For example, let's assume you are a project manager and below is your work to-do list:

- Clear the backlog of non-urgent emails in my inbox.

- Finalise the scope and budget for a new project kicking off in two weeks-time.

- Catch-up meeting to discuss feedback from a project that finished one month ago.

- Discuss a concern raised with you in the last 12 hours about the well-being of a team member.

- Review current project – over budget, payment to a supplier delayed and supplier stopped working on project until payment received.

If you were to start your day at the top of the list, e.g., clear the backlog of emails, it's possible that you would still be clearing emails at the end of the day and at most moved onto the next thing on your to do list. Whilst one could argue that all things on this list are important, clearly some are your "frogs," or your MITs that are going to have the biggest, positive impact on your outcomes right now.

If we take a look at the to-do list, your MITS are likely to be the last two points and these should be prioritised above everything else on your list. And whichever of these is the hardest should be tackled first.

The tasks on your MIT list will stand for at least 80 percent of your output. Focus on the MITs and try to find ways to either eliminate or decrease the amount of time you spend on other tasks.

The MIT prioritisation process can be utilised beyond the work environment; it becomes useful in managing your home priorities, too.

Combining this technique of working on the MIT at the most productive time possible is very effective. And what is enormously effective is to combine it with Parkinson's Law (setting an artificial deadline which is discussed in a later chapter). If you set a goal to finish all your MITs by X time, you'll be surprised how quickly you can complete the day's MITs.

The Eisenhower Urgent/Important Principle

Dwight D. Eisenhower, the 34th President of the United States, developed the urgent/important principle or matrix. The Eisenhower Matrix is a method of determining your MITs and prioritising other things on your to-do list.

Eisenhower's strategy for getting organised and taking action is based on separating your actions by looking at four possibilities defined by four quadrants:

Q1 – Urgent and important (tasks you will do immediately)

Q2 – Important but not urgent (tasks you will schedule to do later)

Q3 – Urgent but not important (tasks you will delegate to someone else)

Q4 – Neither urgent nor important (tasks that you will eliminate)

Eisenhower Matrix

Quadrant 1 tasks are both urgent and important

An urgent task may be a report request from your Manager for a meeting that's currently in progress.

Be mindful of how much time you spend in Q1. If you do spend a lot of time here, you need to question why. Are other people's requests truly urgent and if frequently urgent, is it due to their lack of planning that needs to be addressed?

According to Eisenhower, what is important is seldom urgent and what is urgent is seldom important. Important tasks are things that contribute to our values, goals and desired outcomes.

Quadrant 2 activities (important but not urgent) – we should seek to spend most of our time here

Q2 activities provide us fulfilment and success.

What are some examples of Q2 activities? Here's a sample list:

- Completing a survey on your work team's performance
- Organising a meeting to recognised high performers
- Attending a course on new computer software
- Training for a sporting event
- Learning a new language
- Planning a holiday with family

None of these activities are usually urgent, yet each one of them could be considered to be very important to anyone pursuing them.

There are a number of key challenges to spending enough time and putting energy into Q2 tasks:

- **Knowing what is truly important to you**. If you don't know what specific values and goals matter most to you, you can't determine those tasks you should be focusing your time on in order to reach the desired outcome.

- **Present bias**. We each have a tendency to focus on whatever is perceived as the most urgent at the moment — our default mode. Motivation is a challenge when there is no looming deadline. Departing from this default position requires a good measure of willpower and self-discipline. Where there is no deadline, be sure to set your own short deadline (refer to the chapter Less is More for more guidance).

Given Q2 activities aren't pressing for our immediate attention, they typically keep getting put to the bottom of the pile, as we tell ourselves, "I'll get to those things 'someday' after I've taken care of the urgent things." But 'someday' will never come, if you're waiting for your schedule to clear up a little. You'll always find things to do that make you too busy.

Results of a global six-year study with over 350,000 participants showed there is roughly a 60/40 split of time being spent on important and unimportant tasks. That is, most people spend about 40 percent of their time (that's two working days) doing tasks that don't translate into results or required outcomes. If you can reclaim even a small portion of that 40 percent, you can be amazingly more effective and productive, not to mention you can enhance the quality time you now have for family and friends.

In order to focus on Q2, you need to find time – you need to consciously decide that you are going to make time and that there will be no buts. By making Q2 tasks your top priority, regardless of the emergency, or deadline you're facing, you'll have the mental, emotional, and physical strength to respond positively, rather than react defensively.

Quadrant 3 (Urgent and Not Important Tasks)

Q3 activities require our attention now (urgent), but don't actually help us achieve our goals or fulfil our mission (not important). Most Q3 tasks are requests from other people, helping them reach their own goals and meet their priorities.

Examples of Quadrant 3 activities include most emails, phone calls, text messages or colleagues coming to your desk during your golden hour to ask a favour (more to come on your golden hour in the next chapter).

According to Stephen Covey, author of *7 Habits of Highly Effective People*, many people spend most of their time on

Q3 tasks, thinking they're working in Q1. There's a feeling of importance as Q3 tasks do help others out. They are also usually tangible tasks, which give that sense of satisfaction as you complete them. It feels empowering to check something off your list, but how does that help you achieve your outcomes?

While Q3 tasks help others, they don't necessarily help you. They need to be balanced with Q2 activities. Otherwise, you'll end up feeling like you're accomplishing a lot from day-to-day, but eventually, you'll realise that you're failing to make any progress when it comes to your own medium to long-term goals.

Quadrant 4 – Not Urgent and Not Important Tasks

Quadrant 4 activities aren't urgent and aren't important. They are primarily distractions. They include scrolling through social media, mindlessly surfing the web or watching TV. Aim to spend no more than 5 percent of your time in this quadrant.

By investing time in Q2's activities, you can eliminate much of the issues of Q1, balance the requests of Q3 with your own needs, and enjoy the time-out of Q4, feeling that you've earned Q4.

Don't Prioritise the Week While You're in It – a Perfect Friday Task

Lots of workplaces have team meetings on Monday mornings to prioritise and plan for the week ahead. But, having a meeting on a Monday for the current week isn't nearly as effective as doing it ahead of time – on a Friday. Friday is a perfect day to talk about the coming week. You can reflect on what you accomplished over the previous week, what you want to accomplish in the next week, and you can think about what strategies you'll use to achieve that.

In addition to holding team meetings to prioritise the week ahead, you can denote Fridays as a perfect day for individual planning and prioritisation. Schedule an hour appointment with yourself for figuring out how to progress, track, research, strategise, or conduct any of those "thinking tasks" that normally take a back seat.

Like most, I was a Monday morning team catch-up person, but now I have made the switch to Friday. This has provided effective use of an otherwise ineffective Friday afternoon. Planning and prioritising on this day versus Monday provides clarity for a productive and effective week ahead.

By using the concept of the "Most Important Task", the Eisenhower Urgent/Important Principle and utilising Fridays to plan ahead you'll more effectively prioritise your tasks.

? Do you know what your most important tasks are?

? Are you focused on your most important tasks?

? Referring to the Eisenhower Matrix what quadrant do you spend most of your time in? Is this serving you well?

? What day of the week do you have team meetings and time for personal reflection? Could you benefit from making a change?

1. 🧠 Think through how your daily routine needs to change in order to allow scheduling your MITs before you leave the office each day. And whatever change is required, take action immediately.

2. 🗒 Write down your MITs for the following day before you leave the office each day. Remember, this is a new habit that may take time to form and it may be hard at first so don't quit when you are almost there.

3. ◎ Manage your daily schedule as much as possible so that your MITs can be the first thing you do each day. And just do it!

4. 🗒 Take a list of your daily tasks (mapped out in either the Managing your Energy Levels or Less is More chapter action steps ▶) and identify if they are in Q1, Q2, Q3 or Q4 of the Eisenhower Matrix. If you have a sub-optimal balance, i.e., little in Q2 and a lot in the

other quarters, then reassess what needs to change. Note down what needs to change and when and how you'll go about it.

5. ◎ Be consistent with your new behaviour until it becomes a habit.

You have learned how to prioritise tasks, now is there anything you can do in order to manage your energy levels?

Let's find out...

Managing Your Energy Levels

"Almost everything will work again if you unplug it for a few minutes... including you." (Anne Lamott)

Have you ever known anyone who seems to have boundless amounts of energy? What makes them different? Are they really different?

People who seem to have limitless energy prioritise their peak energy time very well, and they know when to take breaks better than others. Their perceived higher energy levels provide a real advantage of getting through more in a shorter time. But the truth is we all have the potential to realise this advantage, if we can learn how to better manage our energy levels, how to renew the human energy resource.

Our energy levels are also influenced by what we eat, caffeine consumed, sleep patterns, how hard we work, and a whole lot more. Energy capacity diminishes with both over-use and under-use. Understanding how our energy fluctuates throughout the day will allow a balance between energy consumption and energy renewal.

Know Your Golden Hours and Energy Dips

Everyone has golden hours, or biological prime time, the key windows of time that you are at your peak. Your golden hour or biological prime time is when you're at your peak: you're alert, ready to be productive, and intent on crossing things off your to-do list.

A crucial part of managing your energy level is maximising productivity during your peak energy time.

However, before you can maximise your biological prime time or golden hours, you need to understand exactly when that time is. If you aren't aware of this time, here's a suggestion to help.

Set up a spreadsheet (example below) or create a paper form to log your daily activity (both work and non-work hours). When possible, log your energy, motivation, and focus levels every two hours while awake during a two to three-week working period. Give each time period recorded a rating from one to ten. A more accurate log will result if you can resist caffeine, alcohol, and any other mood enhancers or depressants during this period. If this is not possible, ensure you note on your log when you have used a mood enhancer like caffeine. Also, note when and what you eat; keep in mind that your energy will dip because of sugary, unhealthy foods that spike your blood sugar and then lower it.

Logging your energy levels can be tedious, but you'll be rewarded with productivity gains after analysing the results.

Date	Time	Energy rating	Motivation rating	Focus Rating	Time of and last food/ caffeine intake
5 Sept	8 am	8	7	10	7 am cereal, toast, coffee
5 Sept	10 am	10	7	10	-
5 Sept	Noon	8	6	6	-
5 Sept	2 pm	6	6	6	1 pm sandwich, fruit
5 Sept	4 pm	4	4	4	-
5 Sept	6 pm	4	4	4	-
5 Sept	8 pm	2	2	2	7 pm dinner
6 Sept	8 am	9	8	9	7 am cereal, toast, coffee

After two to three weeks of keeping your log, you should see trends during your day. Whenever your energy, focus, and motivation align at a high point, you've found a biological prime time or golden hour. Energy spikes, however, aren't a good thing when they're followed by a crash (like when you've consumed a lot of caffeine or sugar).

Once you find your best time, protect it with all your might; this frees you up to do your best, uninterrupted work. Where possible, block the time out in your calendar as often as you can and use these high-energy hours for your highest priority tasks (your most important tasks) – which often require more mental energy and focus.

Once you have a sense of your prime time, you can then mould your schedule so that the activities you need less energy for (e.g. checking emails) are scheduled in your low energy times.

Plan to take a break when your energy dips, so you can recharge.

Working All Day Without a Break is Counterproductive – We Need to Renew Our Energy Levels

Whatever the work practice or schedule, our brains are designed to work in roughly the same way – in periods of time following a natural flow of energy peaks and troughs. Known as our ultradian rhythm, discovered by Nathan Kleitman, this energy cycle of 90–120 minutes takes us through different levels of alertness.

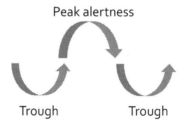

Peak alertness

Trough   Trough

Energy cycle 90-120 minutes
(Ultradian Rhythm)

It's true that our bodies slowly transition from a high-energy state into a physiological trough. The body requires a period of rest and recovery toward the end of each cycle. We all experience the signals it's time to renew; those signals include feeling restless, needing to yawn, feeling hungry, and having difficulty concentrating. However, many of us try to ignore these signals and keep on working. The consequence is that our energy reserves, our remaining capacity to cope, will erode as the day goes on.

Have you ever wondered why something you've been trying to resolve all morning long is magically resolved after a lunch break? This has happened to me many a time.

There have been times when I haven't wanted to stop reviewing an issue until I found the answer, but that answer was a long, long time coming. If I had only known that the answer was on the other side of a short break, I would have taken my break much sooner.

By choosing to work in sync with this natural flow of energy, we can increase our productivity and efficiency by limiting our periods of focus. Intermittent breaks for renewal let us give a more sustainable, increased effort in our activities.

The length of time taken for refreshing ourselves is less important than the quality of that rest. It's possible to gain a great deal of recovery and rest in a short time, if you practice a ritual that allows you to fully disengage from work. In other words, the ritual must allow you to truly switch channels. That positive switch might range from engaging in small talk with a colleague about something other than work, to listening to music, to taking a walk up and down the stairs or around an office building.

While many organisations consider taking breaks to be counter cultural, and they are counter-intuitive for many high achievers, their value is multifaceted.

There are three scientific reasons for prioritising breaks while at work:

1. **Breaks prevent boredom** and make it easier to stay focused. That's because the human brain wasn't built for the type of extended focus, we demand of it all day. The fix for this unfocused condition is easy; all we need to get back on track is a brief interruption.

2. **Breaks assist information retention and forming mental connections**. Our brains have two modes: focused mode (which we use when we're doing things like learning a new skill, writing a document, or working intently) and diffuse mode (which is our more relaxed, day dreamy mode). We are in this mode when we're not actively thinking too hard. Most of us might believe the focused mode will help us optimise productivity but being in diffuse mode is critical in balancing how our brain works.

    We used to believe our brains went dormant when daydreaming. However, recent studies show just the opposite; there is increased activity in many brain regions when we allow our minds to wander. Some studies have shown something very interesting happens that we wouldn't expect, but you've most likely experienced: the mind solves its toughest problems while daydreaming. While you're in the shower or driving along, you may suddenly resolve an issue. Breakthroughs seemingly coming from nowhere can often result from diffuse mode thinking. Diffuse mode thinking occurs when you are taking a true break.

3. **Breaks help us re-evaluate our goals**. What happens is this: when you concentrate on a task continuously, it's easy to lose focus. You get lost as you're pulled into

the details of the work in front of you. In contrast, if you stop for a brief break, you can pick up right where you stopped before. This forces you to spend a little time thinking holistically about your project. You begin to ask yourself if you're on the right track to getting the work done. A break encourages you to be mindful of your true objectives.

What doesn't get planned usually doesn't get done, so make sure to plan for breaks. Better still, make them a habit – then they will just happen.

By doing your most important tasks during your golden hour, you'll achieve more of what you want in a shorter period of time. And by taking a break which triggers the diffuse mode thinking, you'll solve difficult problems in no time.

?   Do you know your golden hour/biological prime time?

?   Do you manage your day so that you use your prime time for high priority tasks, and down time for less mentally challenging tasks?

?   How often do you have a break throughout the day?

?   How can you introduce more breaks into your day and make them a habit?

1.   ☑ Log your daily activity to determine your prime time for two to three weeks based on the template suggested in the chapter.

2.   ☑ When you know your prime time, spend some time thinking about how your day is structured and what needs to change to maximise your prime time. Note down the changes required.

3.   ◎ Restructure your daily calendar where possible to ensure you are doing high value things in your prime time and low value things in your down time. And do this every day in order to make it a habit.

4.   ◎ If you don't have scheduled breaks in your day, take action today and schedule them. Then practice taking breaks until it becomes a habit.

5.   ☺ If you are part of a team, why not discuss the above with them? Then, they will have some background

when you change your schedule to maximise your prime time and they will understand the importance of scheduling a break so that they too can make a positive change.

Now that you know how to manage your energy levels, let's discuss one of the most important reasons for becoming a more life-work balanced person...

Why This One Family Ritual Must be Given Priority

"It's not about having time. It's about making time."

If you have a family to get home to at night, then this chapter will be particularly important to you. If you don't have a family to go home to you can substitute this family ritual for whatever is your main reason for wanting to get home whether that be for dinner with friends, exercising or just a relaxing night on the couch.

What is this "one family ritual" that is so important?

Having dinner with family ...

Before we get into why it's so important, let's first cover the cost of working too much overtime.

Staying late to meet a deadline or deliver a product on time will occasionally be necessary, but for many, working overtime is the accepted norm and an unhealthy habit. There are a number of reasons for overtime:

- It's required, just to keep up with the amount of work that has to be done.

- Company culture (or perceived culture) supports the idea that those who work longer hours will be promoted more quickly for working "harder."

- Team members want to mimic the hours of a manager. Many managers arrive at the office earlier and depart later than others each day. Their team may mimic their schedule, because they believe working longer hours is necessary to gain approval.

- The manager expects their team to work longer hours to demonstrate commitment.

Loads of research has proven beyond a doubt that excessive, routine overtime does not, in and of itself, increase productivity. The small bump in extra output you might achieve by staying later is often more than offset by your decreased energy and resultant effectiveness for the rest of the week. For example, if you stay late on Monday night to get something done at work, your Tuesday is going to be much less productive than normal. And by the end of the week, working overtime will not have netted any more output than a week where you leave on time each day.

Whether you are working overtime regularly just to keep up with the workload, or due to the other cultural reasons noted above, you can change. Think about how your life would change if you could pick your children up from school one day a week or more, make that exercise class with friends, work on a passion project or simply be home to have dinner with your family or friends.

The productivity tips and tools in this book will allow you to improve your output, helping you get the work done. This alone will not make all the difference, however. You need to believe that it is more than okay to leave the office on time or perhaps earlier and make the conscious choice to honour what is truly important to you. You can have it all!

If the Chief Executive Officer of Intel or Chief Operating Officer of Facebook can avoid overtime, you can too.

In his book, *High Output Management*, the late Andy Grove described how in his days as CEO of Intel he always arrived to work by eight in the morning, but never left later than six – and never took work home with him! Despite all the challenges of leading a giant, fast-growing tech company, Grove says he always kept a schedule that allowed him to be home for dinner. Grove explains his scheduling secret this way: "My day ends when I'm tired and ready to go home, not when I'm done. I am never done. Like a housewife or househusband, a manager's work is never done. There is always more to be done, more that should be done, always more than can be done."

Facebook Chief Operating Officer Sheryl Sandberg explains her finish to each working day: "I walk out of the office every day at 5.30 pm so I'm home for dinner with my kids at six, and interestingly, I've been doing that since I had kids." She goes on to say, "I did that when I was at Google, I do it at Facebook, but I would say it's not until the last two years that I'm brave enough to talk about it publicly. I certainly wasn't running around giving speeches on it."

To make up for leaving work at 5.30 pm, Sandberg said early on she would send emails to her colleagues during late hours at night and very early in the morning. This served as proof she was still totally committed to her work. She says, "I was showing everyone I worked just as hard. I was getting up earlier to make sure they saw my emails at 5.30 am, staying

up later to make sure they saw my emails late. But now I'm much more confident in where I am and so I'm able to say, 'Hey! I am leaving work at 5.30.' And I say it very publicly, both internally and externally." Sandberg is sending a much-needed message that it's okay to leave work before dark.

Having overly full schedules for both parents and children does make it difficult to actually have family dinners. But, if you become aware of the benefits from regularly eating together at the table, you may try harder to do so.

Research points to the fact that having dinner together as a family a minimum of four times a week has positive effects on child development and well-being.

In 2010, a study was published entitled, "The Importance of Family Dinners," by Columbia University's National Center on Addiction and Substance Abuse. Researchers found that teenagers who actually sat down to enjoy dinner with their families, regularly, were better students. They were twice as likely to receive grades in school within the A and B range. In addition, these students were three times more likely to say they had a great relationship with their parents. These same teenagers also had fewer experiences with substance abuse and were documented to be less prone to experiencing any type of eating disorder.

In a New Zealand study, a higher frequency of eating meals with their families was strongly associated with positive moods in teenagers. Similarly, other researchers have concluded that teenagers who dine with their families on a regular basis also enjoy a more positive view of the future, compared to their peers who don't eat with their parents.

Furthermore, research shows that conversation at the dinner table enhances vocabulary for young children, even more so than having adults read aloud to them. The researchers documented the number of rare words (those not on a list of the 3,000 most commonly used words) that were used by families while talking at dinner. It was documented that young children learned 1,000 rare words having dinner with their families, compared to only 143 rare words learned from parents reading aloud (not that we are suggesting to not read to your children – that's important too).

Backed up by over twenty years of research, these benefits are shared by Anne K. Fishel, PhD, co-founder of The Family Dinner Project. A professor at Harvard Medical School, she is the author of *Home for Dinner*, in which she notes that it benefits the brain, body and spirit when individuals sit down with family for a nightly meal.

Challenging your working hours will not only benefit your own effectiveness but also has significant benefits for your family. Whether it be the well-being of your family, or equally important, your own well-being, prioritise getting home for dinner as if it was a 6 pm meeting with your most important client: not to be missed!

? What is keeping you in the office that prevents you from having dinner with your family or friends?

? What needs to change, so that you can be home for dinner?

? What action can you take toward leaving work on time today?

1. ☑ Each day for the next week or two, note down what time you leave the office each day and the reason you left the time you did if it was later than your standard hours.

2. ☑ Make a list of things that you would ideally like to accomplish in your home time but just don't get the chance to do due to your work schedule (ensure having dinner with family is one of these if it's not a ritual today).

3. 🐷 Review the list of reasons noted in point one above and challenge yourself whether change is possible in order for you to achieve your home time list in point two above.

4. 😶 Develop your change plan and discuss with your manager if needed – be sure to comment on the importance of having mealtimes with family.

5.   ◎ Take the first step to change. Do it consistently to
     make it a habit.

Now the question is, what else can you do in order to create
more time?

Let's find out...

Part 3 – Managing Your Time Thieves

Time is your most precious commodity. You can always make more money, learn more, or get more toys. But you'll never be able to get more time.

Time is precious...

And if you had a thief in the night come and steal something from you, you would do almost everything you could to prevent that from happening again. And yet, time thieves are all around us, stealing time from us, and what do we do?

Usually, nothing.

Until now...

In Part 3, Managing Your Time Thieves, you're going to be more conscious of your time thieves as well as learn many tools and techniques in order to keep those time thieves from stealing your most precious commodity – time.

First, let's start with multi-tasking...

Why You Must Stop Conscious Multi-Tasking

"The art of messing up several things at once."

You're working on a complex project at work as a project manager. While deep into your project management software, assigning different tasks to different team members, you get a text, then a phone call, then an email, and then a co-worker interrupts you to talk about a new problem that just came up. You try to respond to all these methods of contact while managing your project because you consider yourself to be a multi-tasker who can handle it.

You may think that those kinds of interruptions are just part of the job and not harmful to your focus, performance and productivity. But if you think that, think again.

Multi-tasking, many would argue, is a necessity in the face of all the demands we need to juggle in today's society. In our highly connected and fast-paced world, we are constantly flooded with information. It's not unusual to be answering emails, phone calls, and texts almost simultaneously. Of course, you want to reply to all instantaneously, but you'll pay a price.

Multi-tasking is a physiological impossibility, unless you happen to be in the one to two percent of the population who are "supertaskers" and use different parts of their brain to divide attention. Your brain most likely can only concentrate on one thing at a time. When you try to accomplish two tasks simultaneously, your brain doesn't have the capacity to complete both tasks successfully.

Experiments have demonstrated that the problem doesn't arise from doing two things at once, so much as doing two separate, conscious mental tasks at once. This results in a significant drop in performance. Completing multiple tasks is possible without impacting performance – if all but one of the tasks are done subconsciously (habitually). For example, when you drive a car you are multi-tasking – but using the accelerator, braking, and putting your indicator on are routine tasks for an experienced driver. This is very different if you are learning to drive, though. A learner driver hasn't been driving long enough for any of the tasks related to driving a car to be done subconsciously. For instance, if the first task is accelerating, and a learner driver then needs to put their indicator on, it is likely they will initially either take their foot off the accelerator or put it down too hard when needing to multi-task. Each time they add a task, their performance will be impacted.

Outlined below are the many issues with multi-tasking:

- **Finite attention span-**When it comes to having an attention span and the ability to be productive, our brains have a finite capacity. Contrary to popular belief, our brains are not wired for multi-tasking well. It's like a pie chart with one section much larger than the others; whatever we're working on will consume most of that pie. There isn't a lot left over for additional tasks, with the exception of automatic behaviours or subconscious tasks such as walking. Switching back and forth between several tasks actually reduces productivity, and wastes time. This is due to the fact that your attention is expended on the act of switching gears – plus, the reality is that you never get fully "in the zone" for either activity. Experts estimate that switching between tasks can cause up to a 40 percent loss in productivity.

- **Bad brain habits-**This constant switching back and forth on tasks encourages bad brain habits. When we finish a small activity (sending an email, answering a text message), we are hit with a dollop of dopamine, which is our reward hormone. Our brains love that dopamine, so we're tempted to keep switching back and forth between mini tasks that provide lots of instant gratification. This leads to a dangerous feedback loop. This situation makes us feel like we're accomplishing a lot, but the truth is, we're not really doing much at all (at least nothing that requires much critical thinking).

- **Organising thoughts-**Stanford researchers compared various groups of people in a study based on individuals' tendency to multi-task and each person's belief that multi-tasking helps their performance. Researchers discovered that people who heavily multi-task – those who engage in it often, and feel this practice enhances their performance – were actually worse at multi-tasking than others who preferred to accomplish one thing at a time. The frequent multi-taskers performed worse because this group had more trouble organising their thoughts. They also had trouble filtering out irrelevant information, in addition to being slower at switching from a given task to another.

- **Inattentional blindness-**People who are busy trying to do two or more things at once don't even see obvious things that are clearly apparent to others. We witness this every day, particularly given the addiction to mobile phones. According to a study from Western Washington University, 75 percent of college students who were observed walking across a campus square and simultaneously talking on their cell phones failed to notice a nearby clown riding a unicycle. Researchers refer to this as "inattentional blindness," saying that despite the fact that individuals using phones were technically looking at their surroundings, none of it actually registered in their brains. This may have been okay in the case of not seeing the clown, but it can have more serious consequences in the workplace and in society generally.

- **Short-term memory-**It makes sense that if you try to accomplish two things at the same time, such as read a book and watch television, you will miss important details of one or both activities. But even stopping one task to suddenly concentrate on another can be sufficient to disrupt one's short-term memory.

- **Creativity-**Multi-tasking utilises working memory, or temporary brain storage. When your working memory is fully used up, it can subtract from your ability to think creatively, according to research from the University of Illinois at Chicago. Researchers suggest that, with too much activity already going on in their minds, multi-taskers will often find it difficult to daydream and generate spontaneous "ah-ha" moments.

- **Handling each thing multiple times-**OHIO is an acronym for "only handle it once," meaning you take something on and don't quit until you've completed it. The problem with multi-tasking, however, is that it generally makes OHIO impossible – instead, you're handling each thing multiple times. And every time you do, you'll be psychologically switching gears. This constant switching requires as much time for you to resume performing a major task that has been interrupted as you've spent working on it, if not more. In their book, *The Cost of Not Paying Attention: How Interruptions Impact Knowledge Worker Productivity*, Jonathan Spira and Joshua Feintuch state that more than 25 percent of every 9 to 5 workday is taken up by such interruptions.

- **Lowering IQ temporarily-**Multi-tasking makes it more difficult to get your thoughts organised, and it's harder to filter out irrelevant information. This reduces the efficiency and quality of anyone's work. Research reveals that in addition to slowing down your efforts, multi-tasking lowers your IQ temporarily. A study at the University of London found that participants who multi-tasked during cognitive tasks experienced IQ score declines similar to what they'd expect if the subjects had smoked marijuana or stayed up all night. IQ drops of fifteen points for people multi-tasking ended up lowering their scores to the average range of an eight-year-old child. So, the next time you're writing an email to your manager during a meeting, keep in mind that your cognitive capacity is being diminished significantly; you might as well let an eight-year-old write the email for you.

- **Increase in the stress hormone-**Multi-tasking has also been proven to increase the production of cortisol, referred to as the stress hormone. Having your brain constantly switch gears pumps up our stress level and tires you out, causing you to feel mentally exhausted (despite the fact the workday has barely begun).

One of the biggest impacts of multi-tasking mayhem comes from your inbox. Some studies demonstrate that even having the potential opportunity to multi-task, such as thinking about an unread email in your inbox, can lower your effective IQ by ten points! Having the constant thrill of a new, bolded email in your inbox can keep you perpetually distracted.

Email is problematic, but texting is even worse. Texting demands much more immediacy than email, tempting you to check it more often. How many hundreds of touches a day does your mobile or cell phone receive?

Multi-tasking is certainly not a skill one should include on a resume; instead, it should be considered a bad habit that one should put a stop to. We all need to turn off notifications on our computers and phones, create specific times to check email during the day, and put our focus on the task before us.

Refer to the chapters on prioritisation, habits, focus and managing your inbox for tips on how to move away from multi-tasking.

I'm a self-confessed multi-tasker, or I was. After doing research for this book, I started to notice things I do and how multi-tasking is letting me down. I am changing, but the change takes time. There are years of the task-switching habit that I need to change. The change to date, however, has had significant, and immediate, positive impact on my productivity.

?   Are you conscious of when you multi-task and notice how it impacts your performance?

?   Can you consciously reduce multi-tasking, one task at a time?

?   Can you use the ideas from the chapter on focus to help you make the shift away from multi-tasking?

1. ☑ Spend some time thinking about your daily and weekly routine and when you consciously multi-task (distinct from unconsciously multi-task which is ok). Write these down.

2. ☑ Next to each task/item write down the impact you think it is having on your focus, performance and/or productivity. (If you are unable to identify a strong enough impact, a strong enough why, you won't successfully implement a change).

3. 🎤 Agree with yourself what changes you want to make and what you need to do to ensure the change happens. Perhaps create your own penalty system. For example, if you want to stop checking your phone messages whilst in a meeting and you find yourself doing it, you need to deny yourself your daily cup of coffee the next day.

It's rather surprising, right? Multi-tasking actually lowers your IQ temporarily and makes you much less productive. One of the biggest contributors to the multi-tasking problem is email.

Manage Your Inbox So It Doesn't Manage You

"If you ended your day with a lot on your list, you probably started the day with email."(Matt Hudson)

Do you always begin your day reading emails, thinking that you'll only respond to the most important ones – then finally look up and realise an hour or more is gone? Without focused management, our inboxes can take a lot of time and energy, making us feel that we struggle to just keep our heads above water.

On average, each of us spends over a quarter of our day wading through our inbox (28 percent per a McKinsey Global Institute Study). That's a huge opportunity cost on our time.

It's not enough to be efficient with your inbox if your efficiency is ineffective. Efficiency is performing a given task (important or not) in the most economical manner possible. Checking emails thirty times throughout the workday and creating a system of folder rules and sophisticated techniques for ensuring that you move them out of your inbox as quickly as possible may be efficient, but it's far from effective.

> **Efficiency is doing things right. Effectiveness is doing the right things. (Peter Drucker)**

Here are some tips to allow you to manage your inbox more effectively and get significant time back in your day.

- **Turn off your new mail alert** – The intention of the alert is to let you know there is another new email in your inbox. This may have been relevant when there was very little email traffic, if that was ever the case. However, now we all receive emails constantly and consistently through the day. The alert is doing nothing more than highlighting the obvious reality, but it is killing your productivity. Every time you receive an alert, it distracts you from the task at hand, whether you realise it or not. If you make no other change from reading this chapter, just turn off the alert – you'll instantly see a significant difference.

- **Establish a schedule for checking email** – Ensure management of your inbox doesn't expose you to the bad brain habit of multi-tasking by establishing an email schedule. Create a routine of when you will read and act on your emails each day; this could be two, three, or four times a day, perhaps early morning, early afternoon, and a few minutes before business close. Once you create that routine, stick to it. Don't be tempted to review emails outside of your designated times.

  When establishing your email routine, think through the ramifications of checking your emails first thing in the morning. By checking email in the morning, are you allowing email to dictate the rest of your day, instead of deciding for yourself what your most important tasks will be for that day?

If you move to a twice daily routine, you may wish to create an automatic response to let your clients, suppliers, co-workers, and manager know. Don't ask to implement a less-frequent email routine, just do it – beg for forgiveness (although unlikely to be needed), don't ask for permission.

In a case study, an employee drowning in emails due to lack of email management created a ritual of checking his email just twice a day, at 10.15 am and 2.30 pm. Whereas previously he couldn't keep up with all his messages, he discovered he could clear his inbox each time he opened it – the reward of fully focusing his attention on email for forty-five minutes at a time. He also reset the expectations of all the people he regularly communicated with by email. "I've told them if it's an emergency and they need an instant response, they can call me and I'll always pick up," he said. Nine months later, he had yet to receive such a call!

There is also a health-related reason for scheduling email checks. When University of California Irvine researchers conducted an experiment to measure the heart rates of employees with and without continual access to office email, they discovered something very interesting. Those individuals who received a steady stream of messages stayed in a perpetual "high alert" mode, with correspondingly higher heart rates. Employees without constant email access did less multi-tasking and were less stressed because of it!

- **Process messages quickly** – When you open your inbox, process it until you're done. Don't just look at an email and leave it sitting in your inbox. Never put anything in a holding pattern, email or otherwise, if you can avoid it; that's a huge time-waster. Remember OHIO, only handle it once. Don't save an email or a phone call to deal with later. As soon as something gets your attention, you should act on it.

Make it a rule to not leave the inbox with emails hanging around. Work your way from top to bottom, one email at a time. Open each message and take care of it immediately. Remember the four Ds – **Delete, Do, Delegate or Defer**. Your choices:

o   **Delete/Archive** – Be brutal. Keep in mind that if you move email messages to the trash bin, this doesn't instantly wipe them out. Later in the day, if you realise you need a deleted message, you can still retrieve it, if you've not yet emptied the trash bin. Or if you need to keep a message for later reference, archive it.

o   **Do it** – If it requires two minutes or less just do it – act or reply immediately, then archive or delete.

o   **Delegate it** – if someone else is the best person to action the email then forward the email, then archive or delete.

o   **Defer/schedule it** – Put more time-consuming items on your to-do list. Click and drag the email to the calendar, or to your tasks.

Get in and out of the inbox quickly, moving on to the next email. If you practice this enough, you can plough through pages of emails very quickly.

- **If you want to receive less emails, send fewer emails** – It's that simple.

- **Be precise, the shorter the email, the better** – When you write an email, say exactly what you mean; use concise, clear, straightforward language and use as few words as possible. Shorter emails get faster responses. Precision also makes it less likely you'll receive subsequent emails generating confusion. Avoid communicating in ways that lead to lots of follow-up questions, seeking clarity you failed to provide the first time.

- **Be clear on the objective of the email in the subject line and email opener** – The subject line often determines whether an email is opened or not. Ensure the subject line is short and clear and provides details of the email purpose. The subject line or email opener should state whether the email is a request for an action to be taken (and stated deadline) or if it is for information only.

- **Create rules to move specified emails automatically to sub-folders or trash** – You can establish rules to automatically move emails from/to a certain person or move a subject containing particular words to a specified sub-folder. This is useful for all types of emails such as regular reports you want to retain or group emails that you can't unsubscribe to but want to automatically delete.

  A favourite of mine is the meeting acceptance email rule. Most of us don't need to know if someone has accepted (if we occasionally need to know, we can take a look) – only if they have declined or marked the acceptance as tentative. You can set up a rule so that all acceptances automatically go into a certain folder, potentially the trash folder. If you organise a lot of meetings, creation of this rule will reduce the volume of emails significantly.

- **To Cc or not Cc**? – Use the To: and Cc: fields to separate individuals in terms of: who the email message is sent to, denoting that you expect a response from this person or persons, and who is getting the message as a copy only and hence no action or response is required.

   Typically, you will receive back two to three times the number of emails you send. The email proliferation occurs largely because of copying others on your original messages.

   Cc-ing, however, certainly has a purpose. The reasons you may copy others on an email are you were asked to, the message provides relevant information for those receiving it, or recipients may need to review the information and take appropriate action in some manner.

   However, keep in mind that other motives might prompt you to copy recipients unnecessarily. For example, you might copy your manager because you want him or her to know you've followed through on certain tasks. You are sending your communication as proof of your work, which you might not really need to do. Also, it can be tempting to cc a recipient or two simply because it's the normal culture of this type of communication.

   As you begin to reflect on your approach when you copy others on emails, you will likely start to pay attention to your own habits and patterns of cc-ing. You will find that you can streamline your communication methods to cc less and make better use of your time – and even more so of those receiving the emails. Awareness is necessary to save time and energy regarding any work-related task.

- **Use 'reply to all' sparingly** – When you type a reply to an email, remember that you should reply only to recipients who will be directly affected by your communication in the response. This will reduce email traffic and improve communication flow all around.

- **Unsubscribe from unwanted emails** – Be ruthless in unsubscribing. These emails take up a lot of space in your inbox over time, not to mention the wasted effort in deleting them each time they come through.

- **Use groups** – If you mail the same group of people repeatedly, set up a group or email alias. You can save yourself time by not having to type each person's name when you mail the group each and every time.

- **Acknowledge receipt where relevant** – Where relevant, but only where relevant, provide a response to the sender. This lets the sender know you received the message, that you don't require any additional information or context, and therefore, they can check the correspondence off their list. Your response should be short; the fewer words, the better; e.g. "Thanks," "Got it," "Makes sense," etc.

- **Have one calendar** – Have one calendar for all of your appointments in all areas of your life. By doing this, you make it impossible to double-book yourself, and it makes your life simpler.

- **Pick up the phone and make a call**, but also know when face-to-face communication is necessary. When you receive an email with a question that you sense will need a few back and forth messages, pick up the phone or meet face-to-face instead; this may save significant time.

In the article "5 Reasons Why Meeting Face-to-Face Is Best," Craig Jarrow explains the benefits of being able to actually see the colleague you're speaking with. He says that meeting in person gives you the opportunity to perceive and interpret the other person's body language. This includes the individual's facial expressions and posture. It's also true that any type of email exchange might go back and forth several times, and the underlying issue at hand may never be clearly identified. If you're actually having a face-to-face with a colleague, you can see this person react and respond. You can deal with problems in real time and avoid infinite email exchange, which permits you to get right to the centre of any problems at hand.

Of course, not all of these inbox management strategies will work for everyone. Clearly, in some roles, you will have to check emails on a regular basis, especially if your business uses email as its main communication tool. No matter what strategies you deploy, remain focused on reducing the time you spend in your inbox.

? How much time are you spending managing your inbox?

? Do you need to check emails as often as you do? What focus price are you paying?

? What strategies can you implement to reduce the time spent on managing your emails?

1. ☑ Think through then write down what bad email habits you have and hence what needs to change, using the suggestions to better manage your inbox in the chapter as a guide.

2. ☑ Document what the change is and the plan for change. (Refer to the chapter on habits to ensure you are able to make your change lasting and effective.)

3. 💬 Schedule time to set yourself up for success as you make the change. For example, do you need to discuss with team members how you're changing the frequency of checking emails? Or, do you need to setup some emails rules? Or, do you need to ask how to stop the email alert?

4. ◉ Then just do it!

Email isn't the only time thief. Meetings are too. But there are lots of things you can do to keep this thief from stealing your time.

How to Improve the Effectiveness of Meetings

"The magic to a great meeting is all of the work that's done beforehand." (Bill Russell)

Meetings are one of the most significant time investments that organisations make. When you consider the hourly rate of everyone attending, meetings are expensive. You may need to get management approval for a $1,000 expense, but you can call a weekly one-hour meeting with twenty people and no one notices! It's a sneaky time thief that needs to be addressed.

It is the responsibility of leaders to manage the cost of meetings like they would manage other company expenditure. Are you or your leaders shirking this responsibility?

And if you are not a leader, how can you do your part in challenging the status quo?

You may have heard sayings such as:

> **"A meeting consists of a group of people who have little to say – until after the meeting." (Pamela Shaw)**

> **"The least productive people are usually the ones who are most in favour of holding meetings." (Thomas Sowell)**

> **"A meeting is an event at which the minutes are kept, and the hours are lost." (Joseph Stilwell)**

Many productive people don't like meetings because they often feel like meetings don't accomplish much. Most organisations over-rely on meetings. People acknowledge that there are too many meetings, but they don't see an alternative.

Meetings do have a place in every organisation, however. With the right level of attendance, frequency of meetings, pre-work before each one, management in the meeting and post, they are an effective way of conducting a deep intervention into something. However, if any of these factors are missing, the meeting will get in the way of real productivity and the organisation's bottom line.

Below are some tips on how to make meetings effective, rather than a productivity killer:

- **Be very clear about the purpose/objective**. Do you want a decision? Do you want to generate ideas? Is the meeting a status update? Are you communicating something, etc.? Ensure you communicate the purpose/objective clearly.

- **Does the meeting need to happen**? If the anticipated meeting outcomes sound weak, you probably don't need to have the meeting in the first place. People will thank you for time back in their day.

- **Should you trim attendance**? It is likely that the higher the number of people attending, the less effective the meeting. Question why there are two levels of people from the one team in the same meeting. Either the more junior person needs to be empowered to go to the meeting and make decisions, or, the more senior person needs to go alone. Consider and reconsider each person invited.

- **Set an agenda** and ensure it is communicated prior to the meeting.

- **Start the meeting on time**.

- **Stick to the agenda**. Redirect discussion to the relevant points, manage ramblers respectfully but firmly, and ensure that the meeting outcomes are met. Ensure someone is the timekeeper so all things on the agenda are discussed within the allocated time.

- **How long does the meeting need to take**? Could the meeting be wrapped up in half the time? A short meeting is a good meeting. Short meetings mean everyone remains attentive and forces everyone to get to the point quickly. Short meetings mean you have to be a lot more careful as to what the agenda is, and how to make the best use of time.

- **Do you need a conventional meeting room table and chairs for the meeting?** Stand-up meetings are now very popular. Standing means people can't necessarily get too comfortable and hence are motivated to have a shorter meeting.

- **At the end of the meeting, ensure you have clear agreement** – who will do what and by when? It's worth spending the last 5 minutes of the meeting clarifying actions out of the meeting.

- **If the meeting is scheduled longer than ninety minutes**, consider a break mid-meeting to ensure focus remains for the duration of the meeting.

- **End on time**.

- **Take accurate minutes**. Document and share the main points.

- **Question the necessity of recurring meetings**. Too often, weekly or monthly meetings are held simply because they are already on everyone's calendar. Periodically, audit recurring meetings to assess whether or not they should continue as is, be restructured and repurposed, or be removed from your schedule completely. Just because a meeting has occurred in the past does not mean it should continue indefinitely.

A number of companies are taking a different approach to meetings to win back some time in their working week. For example, one company only has meetings one day a week – mad meeting Mondays! On Mondays, they ask everyone to come into the office, meet, discuss, and make decisions. The rest of the week is meeting free, allowing greater flexibility of hours and place of work.

Only having meetings one day a week may appear to be too radical a shift for your organisation. A more realistic schedule may be banning meetings on one day of the week: the "meeting fast." This is something that you as an individual can schedule, even if it isn't necessarily sanctioned company wide. Why not block your diary (not allowing any meetings) one day of the week? The productivity benefits will be immediate.

? How can you improve the effectiveness of meetings using the tips above?

? How can you reduce the time you or your team spend in meetings? What action can you take today?

? Could you or your company have at least one day of the week as a "meeting fast"?

1. 🎤 Acknowledge what is wrong with the meeting culture in your organisation – is it too many meetings without clear purpose, too loose an agenda, too many people attending, too long, or too loose on follow-up?

2. 💬 Whether you are a leader or not within your organisation, develop a proposed "call to action" to change the meeting culture and discuss this with your manager including how you will be part of the "call to action."

3. 🎤 Work with the relevant team to review the guiding principles of meetings and how they can be entrenched and enforced in your organisation, or at the very least, your team.

4. 💬 Be brave enough to call out ineffective meeting practices.

Meetings are a big-time thief. But are there things that we can proactively do in order to be more productive?

Why Less is More

"There is not enough time to do all the nothing we want to do." (Bill Watterson)

Do you ever have days or weeks where you say yes to every request that comes your way without questioning whether it's adding value to anything? And for each of those requests, do you also have no clear time or date for completion? You get to the end of the day/week and have achieved little to nothing. We all have days like this, some of us much more than others.

Understanding and practicing the 80/20 Principle and Parkinson's Law can ensure that you don't get to the end of your day or week and have achieved little to nothing.

The 80/20 Principle and Parkinson's Law are two approaches to heighten productivity, with each being inversions of the other: the 80/20 Principle suggests limiting tasks to the important, so you can decrease work time and Parkinson's Law proposes defining a shorter time span for working to ensure you do restrict tasks to important ones. The best outcomes can be achieved by using both together, whereby you identify the tasks that maximise output and define very short and clear deadlines in scheduling them.

In order to benefit from the 80/20 Principle and Parkinson's Law we need to first learn how to say no.

Learning to Say No – the Hidden Power

> **"You have to decide what your highest priorities are and have the courage pleasantly, smilingly, and non-apologetically – to say "no" to other things. And the way to do that is by having a bigger yes burning inside." (Stephen Covey)**

Our ideas of success for ourselves is often built on an impulsive habit of saying "yes" to opportunities that come our way. We're hungry for any chance to prove ourselves; and when we're presented with one, we take it. We all want to say yes because with yes comes opportunity, but with the power of no comes focus and engagement.

When we think of highly successful people, we naturally think of all the things they do. We reflect on what they are known for, but the reality is that in order for them to be successful, there would be a long list of things that they didn't do, that they said "no" to along the way.

By saying yes to too many things, we may also be saying no to some very important things.

When you feel pressured to say yes but know that you should turn down an opportunity or request with a polite no, remind yourself of the reason behind your decision. You are not a failure if you say no. Saying no to a new commitment honours your existing commitments and maximises the opportunity to make your current responsibility or obligation a success.

Not knowing how to say no inevitably results in over-commitment. You wind up with a sub-standard outcome, personally exhausted and potentially hamper your reputation in the process. Research conducted at the University of California shows that the greater difficulty you have with saying no, the more likely you are to experience stress, burnout, and potentially depression.

It is important to say no gracefully but firmly, maintaining the relationship with someone, while making it clear that this is one opportunity you're choosing not to pursue. Be clear on the rationale for your decision, being as transparent as possible.

There's no magic method for saying no effectively. The key is practice, practice, practice. Saying no is like any other interpersonal skill: it feels hard, clumsy and awkward at first, and improves only with repeated effort.

The 80/20 Principle – More Effectively Using Your Time

> **"Deciding what not to do is as important as deciding what to do." (Steve Jobs)**

An Italian economist, Vilfredo Pareto, founded the Pareto principle, now known as the 80/20 Principle, in 1897. Pareto observed that 80 percent of the land in Italy (and every country he subsequently studied) was owned by 20 percent of the population. Pareto's theory of predictable imbalance can be applied to almost every aspect of modern life.

Richard Koch took Pareto's Principle and applied it to business, productivity, and life. The essence of the 80/20 principle is that 20 percent of your effort accounts for 80 percent of your results. Conversely, you can apply this theory to become aware of the 80 percent of your efforts that yield only 20 percent of your accomplishments.

IBM was one of the earliest corporations to use the 80/20 Principle. In 1963, IBM discovered that about 80 percent of a computer's time was spent executing about 20 percent of the operating code. The company immediately modified its operating software to make the most used 20 percent very accessible and user friendly, thus significantly increasing the speed and efficiency of IBM computers relative to their competitors.

There are loads of business examples of the 80/20 Principle. This includes realising that 80 percent of a company's output is achieved by 20 percent of its employees, and 80 percent of a company's revenues come from 20 percent of its customers. It won't be exactly 80/20, but it is highly probable in business that a minority is creating a majority. It may be roughly 90/10, 70/30 or 60/40.

The 80/20 ratio applies to both your workday and your life outside work. You probably make most of your phone calls to, or spend most of your time with, a limited amount of the people you have numbers for and know. You probably wear 20 percent of your wardrobe 80 percent of the time. And, the majority of the times you eat out, you probably dine at the same 20 percent of the restaurants you know.

The 80/20 Principle suggests that there is a huge amount of waste everywhere and asserts that there is no shortage of time, given we only make effective use of 20 percent of our time. The 80/20 Principle says that if we doubled our time on the top 20 percent of activities, we could achieve 60 percent more in much less time.

The 80/20 Principle: The Secret to Achieving More with Less by Richard Koch talks about the top ten low value uses of time:

1. Things other people want you to do
2. Things that have always been done this way
3. Things you're not usually good at doing
4. Things you don't enjoy doing
5. Things that are always being interrupted
6. Things few other people are interested in
7. Things that have already taken twice as long as you originally expected
8. Things where your collaborators are unreliable and low quality
9. Things that have a predictable cycle
10. Answering the telephone/responding to emails

The idea is that much related to the above ten items makes up about 80 percent of your day, and only contributes to 20 percent of your results. You can only spend time on high-value activities, the 20 percent, if you no longer spend time on low-value uses of time. So, in order to boost your productivity, you must eliminate or substantially reduce the time you spend on the above.

Do you know what you spend your hours in the office doing? Studies and data have shown that how we think we spend our time has little to do with reality. You can gain more control over your time and your work by taking one small step right now. Challenge yourself to understand what you spend 80 percent of your time on. Simply begin to look for the signs that will tell you whether you're in your 20 percent or your 80 percent. You may want to document what you do, hour by hour, for a few weeks (perhaps you could combine this with the daily activity log suggested in the chapter on Managing your Energy) to obtain clarity on your 80/20.

There is no more effective way to reduce the time taken to complete a task in your 80 percent than not doing it at all.

Create a "Stop doing" List. Too often, productivity, time management, and prioritisation mean we avoid the real question of whether we actually need to be doing the task at all. It's often much easier to remain busy, to work a little later on a given night than step out of your comfort zone of eliminating a task. Often, you'll have grown comfortable with doing a task, regardless of whether it's the best use of your time. As Tim Ferriss, self-help author and speaker says, "Being busy is a form of laziness – lazy thinking and indiscriminate action."

Be strong and make decisions to delete any task not leading you toward your values and your goals. **A "stop doing" list is as important as a "to-do" list.** By understanding what to stop doing, you can focus on the high-value items that should take up the most productive 20 percent of your time, which are, according to Richard Koch:

1. Things that advance your overall purpose in life
2. Things you have always wanted to do

3. Things already in the 20/80 relationship of time to results
4. Innovative ways of doing things that promise to slash the time required and/or multiply the quality of results
5. Things other people tell you can't be done
6. Things other people have done successfully in a different arena
7. Things that use your own creativity
8. Things that you can get other people to do for you with relatively little effort on your part
9. Anything with high-quality collaborators who have already transcended the 80/20 rule of time, who use time eccentrically and effectively
10. Things for which it is now or never

Parkinson's Law – Work Expands to Fill the Time Available for It

> **"The more things you do, the more you can get done." (Lucille Ball)**

Parkinson's Law is the adage that "work expands so as to fill the time available for its completion," which means that if something is due next week, you will likely use the time allotted and the work will only be finished next week. For example, if you're given two months for the same work, then the work will take two months to complete. You will mentally be "pacing" yourself based on the time you have, so even if you want to work faster, it will be mentally challenging.

Cyril Parkinson, a British historian, first observed the trend during his time with the British Civil Service. He noted that as bureaucracies expanded, they became more inefficient. He then applied this observation to a variety of other circumstances, realising that as the size of something increased, its efficiency dropped. He found that even a series of simple tasks increased in complexity to fill up the time allotted to the outcome. As the length of time allocated to a task became shorter, the task became simpler and easier to solve.

Well-known terms are the outcome of Parkinson's Law: If you wait until the last minute, it only takes a minute to do; work contracts to fit in the time we give it; the amount of time that one has to perform a task is the amount of time it will take to complete the task; and the demand upon a resource tends to expand to match the supply of the resource.

Parkinson's Law is the reason you may hear people say, "If you want something done, ask a busy person," even though this idea is somewhat paradoxical.

You are forced to complete tasks in a given time, if you are experiencing time pressure. When there is no pressure attached to a task, it will take longer to complete. In fact, the longer you have to complete the task, the longer it will take you. And, your perception of the importance of a task is influenced by the time allocated. A task that needs completion within a day isn't perceived as important, but a task that's to be finished in two months will be. Perceptions of complexity are also related to the allocated time. The more time your mind thinks it will take will cause you to perceive the task as overly complex and difficult. Waste thrives on complexity; effectiveness requires simplicity.

Per Timothy Ferriss in his book, *The 4-Hour Work Week*: "The world has agreed to shuffle papers between 9 am and 5 pm, and since you're trapped in the office for that period of servitude, you are compelled to create activities to fill that time. Time is wasted because there is so much time available.

Since we have eight hours to fill, we fill eight hours. If we had fifteen, we would fill fifteen; however, if we had an emergency and needed to suddenly leave work in two hours, but had pending deadlines, we would miraculously complete those assignments in two hours."

If you truly focused intently, how long do you think it would take you to finish a day's worth of work? Do you think you could be done in six hours instead of eight? Maybe four? The problem is that if you have to stay until 5 pm or later, there really isn't a way for you to find out.

My early working years, and then the years to follow with young children, were spent practicing Parkinson's Law at its best. I gave myself very short deadlines due to my time constraints, and I also requested short deadlines from those around me to coincide with my time frames. The result was that everything got done and more, in a very short time frame. If I had more time to get the work done, I don't necessarily think more would have been done.

You may be able to relate to this when you are preparing to go on holidays – you have so much to do at work and at home but so little time to do it, with your holiday deadline looming. Magically you get through it all. You are practicing Parkinson's law!

Today, when I create self-imposed deadlines, the relevant activity/task gets done in a very short time frame. It becomes a game, a competition against the clock that I must win, and I do!

Use Parkinson's Law to Your Advantage:

- **Embrace deadlines and constraints**. Force yourself to work against the clock.

- **When you are given a task without a deadline, set the deadline yourself**. I often set a deadline that I need to finish a task by 10 am, another task by 11 am, and a third task by 12 noon. I even use this principle at home; for example, I need to complete the ironing in a certain time. Without doubt, I complete the task (in this example, the ironing) in a shorter period of time with no risk to the quality of the finished product. You will be surprised how a deadline motivates you into action and amazed how productive you can become.

- **Always state a deadline when you delegate** a task to someone else.

- **Deadlines should be as immediate as possible** and time constraints as short as workable. The more time pressure you feel, the more focused you will be and the more work you can complete.

- **Blackmail yourself**: Get an accountability partner who will force you to pay up if you don't meet your deadline.

Cut your work hours in half when you sit down to plot out your day. It'll force you to be extremely picky when it comes to the tasks you agree to take on or contribute to, and it'll give you time to make sure these high priorities actually get done on time.

The overarching lesson from Parkinson's Law is that restrictions can actually create freedom. How can you add artificial parameters to your life and work, in order to become more productive and more prolific and to operate on a bigger scale?

If you implement the concepts from the 80/20 rule, Parkinson's Law, and other methods to stop doing the things that aren't important, you will gain much more time-freedom. And when you make it all become a habit, you'll become a master of efficiency.

Less is more.

?   Are you saying yes to tasks or opportunities you should be saying no to? When was the last time you said yes, but you should have said no? What needs to change next time?

?   How can you make a shift to feeling okay about saying no?

?   Do you know what your 80/20 is? What tasks are you spending most of your time on that are only delivering you very little benefit – both at home and at work? Would documenting your day help you understand your 80/20?

?   What needs to go on your "stop doing" task list?

?   What changes are you going to make today to give you more time and increase your output?

?   Experiment with setting tough deadlines and note the difference and enforce the same on others.

?   Use the spare hours from getting the job done quicker to get out of the office and have fun!

Learning to say no

1. ◉ Each time you are asked to take on a new task/project make it a habit (yes, your world is merely a sum of your habits) to stop and think – should you say yes or no and/or ask for time to consider it. Catch yourself each time you say yes and should have said no.
2. ◉ Repeat no. 1 – practice, practice, practice.

Understanding your 80/20 and taking action

1. ☑ For one or ideally two weeks, write down what tasks/activities you do in 30-minute increments. At the end of each day, note down against each documented task whether it was a high value or low value use of your time (refer to the top 10 high or low value uses of time as listed in this chapter).
2. ☛ After the one or two weeks, review your low value uses of time, as documented.
3. ☛ Develop a plan to reduce or, better still, eliminate the low value uses of time and convert to high value tasks.

Stop doing list

1. ☑ Create a stop doing list – next time you update your to-do list, create another list alongside it – the stop doing list.
2. ☛ Prioritise the stop doing list like you would your to-do list (refer to the chapter on prioritisation).
3. ☑ Cross off your stop doing list as you go.

4.   ◎ Repeat 1-3!

Create tight deadlines

1.   🧠 Think about what consumes your hours and days at work and at home and what activities take you longer than the desirable time. What artificial deadlines can you create so tasks get done quicker, with no impact to quality? Set these deadlines now. (you may need to consult the chapter on habits to help you with ensuring this isn't a one off, but a habit.)

2.   🧠 When you next update your to-do list, or more importantly, your Most Important Tasks List, add tight timeframes/deadlines for completion. Be bold and put perhaps what you would consider slightly unrealistic time-frames – you'll be surprised what a deadline will do. And stick to those deadlines.

3.   ◎ If someone gives you a project/task and provides a deadline, there is no need to question the deadline with that person. However, for yourself, question whether or not you need that much time. Also, ask yourself, will I only build complexity in the process if I give myself this long? Is a shorter time period a better use of my time? Challenge yourself and just do it!

Less is more. By putting in 20% of the effort, you'll get 80% of the result. And by giving yourself less time to accomplish something, you'll get more done. It's a paradox, really, that less is more, but it's true. By saying "no" to tasks that do not serve you, you are saying "yes" to doing more for the tasks that matter...

When you start to implement these tactics, you will definitely see that less is more.

Conclusion

I trust you have enjoyed reading this book and you have found it to be useful in attaining a better life-work balance. The truth is that anyone can do it. But first, you have to have the right mindset and the right know-how – the right tools. Perhaps now, you have both.

In this book, we started with the problem of the 40-hour-work week and made the case that it is out-dated and should be fair game to be challenged. We discussed studies that showed that people are actually more productive when they work less, and that they can be more productive when they work from home.

We covered mindset and how important it is to have a powerful desire. Without a powerful desire, you aren't going to be able to muster up the energy necessary to change. We discussed beliefs, how limiting beliefs can stop you, but how a powerful self-belief can carry the day. We also covered the topic of happiness, how a happy employee is a more productive employee and things that you can do in order to be happier.

Then we covered the topic of how to focus, how to stop procrastinating, and the most important topic of habits – and how nothing matters if you don't make it a habit.

We discussed the practical application of how to structure your day which involves starting your day well – which actually starts the night before. You learned about how to prioritise your tasks, how to manage your energy levels, and why eating dinner with your family is so important.

In Part 3, you learned about how to manage your time thieves. If you haven't been mindful of the time thieves in your life, then this part could really be valuable to you. There are many time thieves in your life that you don't even think about, such as how multi-tasking reduces productivity. And how email is also so disruptive to productivity. And then there was the discussion of meetings, and how, when they aren't used properly, they can be a very costly time thief.

Finally, we discussed why less is more, how to say no, the 80/20 rule, why it's important to create a "stop doing" list and Parkinson's law.

We are all given the same amount of time – we all have the same 24 hours. You can't really create time – but you can manage what you do or don't do within the time allotted. The bottom line to this whole book is that by consciously taking control of what you do with the precious time that you have, you can have it all – you can be balanced and happy in life and work.

And that is the gift that I want to give to you…

Thank you for allowing me to share this information with you.

I wish you the best in creating a happier life, allowing you to live, work and SHINE!

References

Web

Feldman, Loren. "Today's Must-Reads For Entrepreneurs: Saving BlackBerry." Forbes. May 23, 2016.http://www.forbes.com/sites/lorenfeldman/2016/05/23/todays-must-reads-for-entrepreneurs-saving-blackberry/.

Bloom, Nicholas. "To Raise Productivity, Let More Employees Work from Home." Harvard Business Review. August 21, 2014.https://hbr.org/2014/01/to-raise-productivity-let-more-employees-work-from-home.

Chung, Frank. "Sweden embraces six-hour workday." News Limited. October 02, 2015.http://www.news.com.au/finance/work/at-work/sweden-embraces-the-sixhour-workday/news-story/567817e54b33509730e2400d04c2dbd9.

Ware, Bronnie. "REGRETS OF THE DYING." Bronnieware.com. November 16, 2015.http://bronnieware.com/regrets-of-the-dying/.

Greenfield, Rebecca. "The Six-Hour Workday Works in Europe. What About America?" Bloomberg.com. May 10, 2016.http://www.bloomberg.com/news/articles/2016-05-10/the-six-hour-workday-works-in-europe-what-about-america.

Career Junction. "Shorter Workweek Good For Companies." Career Junction Blog. May 18, 2016.http://www.careerjunction.co.za/blog/?p=32360.

"Ford factory workers get 40-hour week." History.com. http://www.history.com/this-day-in-history/ford-factory-workers-get-40-hour-week.

Alderman, Liz. "In Sweden, an Experiment Turns Shorter Workdays into Bigger Gains." ACQ5. May 20, 2016.http://www.acq5.com/post/in-sweden-an-experiment-turns-shorter-workdays-into-bigger-gains/.

Widrich, Leonhard. "The Origin of the 8 Hour Work Day and Why We Should Rethink It." The Huffington Post. January 07, 2014; updated November 22, 2016.http://www.huffingtonpost.com/leonhard-widrich/the-origin-of-the-8-hour-_b_4524488.html.

Stott, Phil. "Are We Heading for a 6-Hour Workday?" CLS Legal Staffing. May 24, 2016.http://clslegalstaffing.com/articles/are-we-heading-6-hour-workday.

Neese, Brian. "Working Remotely Works." Rivier University Online. October 14, 2015.http://online.rivier.edu/working-remotely-works/.

Writer, TFPP, Robert Gehl, and C.E. Dyer. "Why Democrats' Version of History of Unions Is All Wrong." The Federalist Papers. May 02, 2016.http://thefederalistpapers.org/us/why-democrats-version-of-history-of-unions-is-all-wrong.

Greenfield, Rebecca. "The six-hour workday increases productivity. So will Britain and America adopt one?" The

Independent. June 0 2016.http://www.independent.co.uk/ news/business/the-six-hour-workday-increases-productivity- so-will-britain-and-america-adopt-one-sweden-a7066961. html.

Monks, Kieron. "Introducing the 20-hour work week." CNN. October 28, 2015.http://www.cnn.com/2015/10/28/world/ twenty-hour-work-week/index.html.

Bloom, Nicholas, and Scott Berinato. "To raise productivity, let more employees work from home." TODAYonline. March 21, 2014.http://www.todayonline. com/singapore/raise-productivity-let-more-employees- work-home.

Cole, Samantha. "Working From Home Is Awesome – If You Do It Right." Fast Company. July 07, 2014. https://www.fastcompany.com/3032648/work-smart/ working-from-home-is-awesome-if-you-do-it-right.

Greenfield, Rebecca. "The six-hour workday works in Sweden. But what about in workaholic North America?" Financial Post. May 11, 2016.http://business.financialpost.com/executive/ careers/the-six-hour-workday-works-in-sweden-but-what- about-in-workaholic-north-america.

Steiner, Susie. "Top five regrets of the dying." The Guardian. February 01, 2012.https://www.theguardian.com/lifeand style/2012/feb/01/top-five-regrets-of-the-dying.

Miller, Tessa. "Why We Should Rethink the Eight-Hour Workday." Lifehacker. June 20, 2013.http://lifehacker.com /why-we-should-rethink-the-eight-hour-workday-515742 249.

"ADVO Group interviews Andreas Konig, CEO at TeamViewer." HR PMI Employee Benefit News.http://news.advogroup.co.uk/advo-group-interviews-andreas-konig-ceo-at-teamviewer/.

Henderson, Adam. "Workplace trust for flexible working." Millennial Mindset. April 29, 2016.http://millennialmindset.co.uk/if-you-cant-trust-your-employees-to-work-flexibly-why-hire-them-in-the-first-place/.

Alderman, Liz. "Shorter workdays equal greater efficiency in Swedish experiment." Financial Review. May 23, 2016. http://www.afr.com/news/economy/employment/shorter-workdays-equal-greater-efficiency-in-swedish-experiment-20160522-gp0s8i.

Rosen, Katerina. "The Top 5 Regrets Of The Dying." The Huffington Post. August 03, 2013.http://www.huffingtonpost.com/2013/08/03/top-5-regrets-of-the-dying_n_3640593.html.

Clifford, Catherine. "Why Amazon and other companies are trying 30-hour workweeks." CNBC. September 16, 2016. http://www.cnbc.com/2016/09/16/why-amazon-and-other-companies-are-trying-30-hour-workweeks.html.

Brinkley, Douglas. "The 40-Hour Revolution." Time Inc. March 31, 2003.http://content.time.com/time/specials/packages/article/0,28804,1977881_1977883_1977922,00.html.

Caprino, Cathy. "Five Reasons You're Killing Yourself Working Overtime, and How to Stop." Forbes. April 30, 2015.http://www.forbes.com/sites/kathycaprino/2015/04/30/5-reasons-youre-killing-yourself-working-overtime-and-how-to-stop/.

Fisher, Sharon. "Employees Looking for Better Work-Life Balance." Laserfiche. April 20, 2015.https://www.laserfiche.com/simplicity/employees-looking-for-better-work-life-balance/.

Clark, Dorrie. "Using the 80/20 Principle to Improve Your Productivity and Happiness." Dorie Clark.http://dorieclark.com/using-the-8020-principle-to-improve-your-productivity-and-happiness/.

Bonne, Emily. "How to Prioritize Your To-Dos When Everything's Important." Wrike. July 23, 2015.https://www.wrike.com/blog/how-to-prioritize-when-everythings-important-video/.

McKay, Brett & Kate. "The Eisenhower Decision Matrix: How to Distinguish Between Urgent and Important Tasks and Make Real Progress in Your Life." The Art of Manliness. October 23, 2013.http://www.artofmanliness.com/2013/10/23/eisenhower-decision-matrix/.

Nesdale, Sheldon. "My notes on The 80/20 Principle: The Secret of Achieving More with Less by Robert Koch." LoveBusinessBooks. February 17, 2009.http://www.lovebusinessbooks.com/2009/02/the-8020-principle-the-secret-of-achieving-more-with-less-by-richard-koch/.

Vaccaro, Pamela J. "The 80/20 Rule of Time Management." American Academy of Family Practice Physicians. Family Practice Management, September 2000. http://www.aafp.org/fpm/2000/0900/p76.html.

Radwan, M. Farouk. "Inspirational stories of successful people." To Know Myself.https://www.2knowmyself.com/inspirational_stories_of_successful_and_famous_people.

Cousens, Caleb. "3 Productivity Killers for Bloggers." Social Media Wizard. May 17, 2016.http://www.socialmediawizard.com/2016/05/17/productivity-killers/.

Betterhealth.vic.gov.au. "Breakfast." Department of Health & Human Services, State Government of Victoria, Australia. https://www.betterhealth.vic.gov.au/health/healthyliving/breakfast.

Adams, R.L. "12 Famous People Who Failed Before Succeeding." Wanderlust Worker, https://www.wanderlustworker.com/12-famous-people-who-failed-before-succeeding/.

Forleo, Marie. "The Secret to More Meaning & Adventure W/Chris Guillebeau." Marie Forleo.http://www.marieforleo.com/2014/09/happiness-of-pursuit/.

Moon, Jerred. "If You're Not Failing, You're Not Trying." End of Three Fitness.http://www.endofthreefitness.com/if-youre-not-failing-youre-not-trying/.

Winfield, Chris. "The Ultimate Guide to Becoming Your Best Self: Build Your Daily Routine by Optimizing Your Mind, Body and Spirit." Buffer Inc. September 21, 2015.https://open.buffer.com/daily-success-routine/.

Ciotti, Gregory. "5 Scientific Ways to Build Habits That Stick." 99u.http://99u.com/articles/17123/5-scientific-ways-to-build-habits-that-stick.

Kjerulf, Alexander. "Top 10 Reasons Why Happiness at Work Is the Ultimate Productivity Booster." The Chief Happiness Officer Blog. March 27, 2007.http://positivesharing.com/2007/03/top-10-reasons-why-happiness-at-work-is-the-ultimate-productivity-booster/.

Duffy, Jill. "Get Organized: 11 Tips for Managing Email." PCMag UK. March 5, 2012.http://uk.pcmag.com/e-mail-products /65853/feature/get-organized-11-tips-for-managing-email.

Bradberry, Travis. "10 Harsh Lessons That Will Make You More Successful." Entrepreneur Media, Inc. October 18, 2016. https://www.entrepreneur.com/article/283726.

Lewis, Michael. "Obama's Way." Vanity Fair. October 2012. http://www.aafp.org/fpm/2000/0900/p76.html.

Clear, James. "The 3 R's of Habit Change: How to Start New Habits That Actually Stick." James Clear.http://jamesclear. com/three-steps-habit-change.

Young, Scott H. "18 Tricks to Make New Habits Stick." Lifehack.http://www.lifehack.org/articles/featured/18-tricks-to-make-new-habits-stick.html.

Unstuck.com. "How We Procrastinate (and May Not Even Know It)." Unstuck LLC.https://www.unstuck.com/ how-we-procrastinate/.

Clear, James. "How to Stop Procrastinating by Using the 2-Minute Rule." James Clear.http://jamesclear.com/ how-to-stop-procrastinating.

Babauta, Leo. "The Amazing Power of Being Present." Zen Habits. August 12, 2011.https://zenhabits.net/mindful/.

Wikipedia. "Flow." Modified January 3, 2017.https:// en.wikipedia.org/wiki/Flow_(psychology).

Seiter, Courtney. "The Science of Taking Breaks at Work: How to Be More Productive by Changing the Way You Think About

Downtime." Buffer Inc. March 23, 2015.https://open.buffer.com/science-taking-breaks-at-work/.

Schwartz, Tony and McCarthy, Catherine. "Manage Your Energy, Not Your Time." Harvard Business Review. October 2007 issue.https://hbr.org/2007/10/manage-your-energy-not-your-time.

Bradberry, Travis. "Multi-tasking Damages Your Brain and Your Career, New Studies Suggest." Talentsmart.http://www.talentsmart.com/articles/Multi-tasking-Damages-Your-Brain-and-Your-Career,-New-Studies-Suggest-2102500909-p-1.html.

Wikipedia. "Pygmalion effect." Modified January 6, 2017. https://en.wikipedia.org/wiki/Pygmalion_effect.

Kim, Larry. "Multi-tasking Is Killing Your Brain." Inc.com. July 15, 2015.http://www.inc.com/larry-kim/why-multi-tasking-is-killing-your-brain.html.

Mindtools.com. "Overcoming Procrastination." Mind Tools Ltd.https://www.mindtools.com/pages/article/newHTE_96.htm.

Paech, Gemma. "Why it's time to stop hitting the snooze button." World Economic Forum. January 7, 2015. https://www.weforum.org/agenda/2015/01/why-its-time-to-stop-hitting-the-snooze-button/.

MacMillan, Amanda. "Multi-tasking Is a Don't: 12 Reasons to Stop Doing It." Awaken. June 15, 2013.http://www.awaken.com/2013/06/multi-tasking-is-a-I-12-reasons-to-stop doing-it/.

Spira, Johnathan & Feintuch, Joshua. "The Cost of Not Paying Attention: How Interruptions Impact Knowledge Worker Productivity." Basex. September 2005.http://iorgforum.org/wp-content/uploads/2011/06/CostOfNotPayingAttention.BasexReport1.pdf.

Lifehacker. "5 Rules of Email Management You Should Adopt." Lifehacker UK. February 18, 2015.http://www.lifehacker.co.uk/2015/02/18/5-rules-email-management-adopt.

Kruse, Kevin. "The 3 Secrets to Leaving the Office by 5 O'Clock-Guilt Free." Mujojoma Dioméde. November 10, 2015. https://mujojoma.wordpress.com/2015/11/10/the-3-secrets-to-leaving-the-office-by-5-oclock-guilt-free/.

Ecker, Ddiana. "15Tips for Managing Email Overload at Work." Redbooth. July 15, 2015. https://redbooth.com/blog/managing-email-overload.

Weiner, Jeff. LinkedIn CEO: How I manage my email." Quartz. August 5, 2013.http://qz.com/111891/linkedin-ceo-how-i-manage-my-email/.

Lyttle, J. and Baugh, E. "The Importance of Family Dinners." University of Florida IFAS Extension.http://solutionsforyourlife.ufl.edu/hot_topics/families_and_consumers/family_dinners.shtml.

Du, Frances. "Why You Shouldn't Feel Guilty About Leaving work at 5:00." Culture-ist. October 17, 2012.http://www.thecultureist.com/2012/10/17/work-life-balance-leaving-work-at-5/.

MacMillan, Amanda. "5 Weird Ways Stress Can Actually Be Good for You." Time Inc. August 22, 2014.http://time.

com/3162088/5-weird-ways-stress-can-actually-be-good-for-you/.

Fishel, Anne. "The most important thing you can do with your kids? Eat dinner with them." The Washington Post. January 12, 2015.https://www.washingtonpost.com/posteverything/wp/2015/01/12/the-most-important-thing-you-can-do-with-your-kids-eat-dinner-with-them/.

Donovan, Laura. "Sheryl Sandberg Leaves Work at 5:30 Every day – and You Should Too." Mashable. April 5, 2012.http://mashable.com/2012/04/05sheryl-sandberg-leaves-work-at-530#6UwiP4Ue3aqU.

Gratias, Melissa. "The Intriguing Psychology Behind CC-ing People on Emails." Redbooth. May 26, 2016.https://redbooth.com/blog/email-cc-psychology.

Goop.com. "Why Stress Is Actually Good for Us – and How to Get good at It: A Q&A with Kelly McGonigal." Goop.http://goop.com/why-stress-is-actually-good-for-us-and-how-to-get-good-at-it/.

Quotes

Quotes not taken from above referenced articles are sourced from: https://www.goodreads.com/quotes.

Books

Ferriss, Timothy. *The 4-hour workweek: escape 9-5, live anywhere, and join the new rich*. New York: Crown Publishers, 2009.

Covey, Stephen R. *The 7 habits of highly effective people*. Provo, UT: Franklin Covey, 1998.

Grove, Andrew S. *High output management*. New York: Vintage, 1995.

Fishel, Anne K. *Home for dinner*: mixing food, fun, and conversation for a happier family and healthier kids. New York: American Management Association, 2015.

Koran, Al. *Bring out the magic in your mind*. Wellingborough, Northamptonshire: Thorsons, 1972.

Koch, Richard. *The 80/20 principle*: London: Nicholas Brealey Publishing, 1998

Printed in the United States
By Bookmasters